D1236879

NOLS
Wilderness Mountaineering

SECOND EDITION

0 11557 02861 4

NOLS
Wilderness
Mountaineering

SECOND EDITION

by Phil Powers

A Publication of the National Outdoor Leadership School and

STACKPOLE
BOOKS

Copyright © 2000 by The National Outdoor Leadership School

Published by
STACKPOLE BOOKS
5067 Ritter Road
Mechanicsburg, PA 17055
www.stackpolebooks.com

All rights reserved, including the right to reproduce this book or portions thereof in any form or by any means, electronic or mechanical, including photocopying, recording, or by any information storage and retrieval system, without permission in writing from the publisher. All inquiries should be addressed to Stackpole Books, 5067 Ritter Road, Mechanicsburg, PA 17055.

Printed in the United States
10 9 8 7 6 5 4 3 2 1

Second Edition

Cover photo by Lon Riesberg
Cover design by Caroline Stover

Library of Congress Cataloging-in-Publication Data
Powers, Phil
        p.   cm.
    Includes index
    ISBN 0-8117-2861-7
    1. Mountaineering. 2. Mountaineering—Equipment and supplies.
3. Mountaineering—Safety measures. I. National Outdoor Leadership
School (U.S.) II. Title. III. Title: Wilderness mountaineering.

GV200.P68   1993
796.5'22—dc20

THIS BOOK cannot and does not alert you to all the hazards of the mountains. It is a learning tool and should be read and studied as a supplemental source only. It is not a substitute for professional instruction, an experienced mentor, or, most importantly, the wilderness experience itself. If you decide to participate in the activities described in this book, the risk and responsibility for the outcome are solely yours. No one associated with the publication of this book, including NOLS and Phil Powers, accepts responsibility for any injury or property damage that may result from participation in such activities.

THE NATIONAL OUTDOOR LEADERSHIP SCHOOL

The National Outdoor Leadership School (NOLS) is a private, nonprofit school based in Lander, Wyoming. NOLS branch schools are located in the Rocky Mountains (Wyoming and the Teton Valley), the Pacific Northwest (Washington), the Southwest (Arizona), Alaska, East Africa, Mexico, Canada (the Yukon), and Patagonia (Chile). Since our founding in 1965, we have graduated more than 53,000 students.

Our mission is to be the leading source and teacher of wilderness skills and leadership that serve people and the environment.

Correspondence and catalog requests may be addressed to:

The National Outdoor Leadership School
288 Main Street
Lander, WY 82520-3128
Telephone: (307) 332-5300
www.nols.edu
admissions@nols.edu

ABOUT THE AUTHOR

Phil Powers began climbing in Oklahoma at the age of fifteen. Since then, his achievements have included the first ascent of the difficult Washburn Face of Mount McKinley, the first winter traverse of the Cathedral Group in the Grand Tetons, and Lukpilla Brakk's Western Edge, a Grade VI rock wall in the Karakoram Range. Phil has reached the summits of two 8,000-meter peaks—K2 and Gasherbrum II—without the use of supplemental oxygen. He has been a

NOLS instructor since 1981 and served as the school's chief mountaineering instructor and development director. He is co-director of Jackson Hole Mountain Guides and Mammoth Mountaineering School and president of the American Mountain Guides Association.

ABOUT THE CONTRIBUTORS

Rob Hess has been a mountain guide and instructor since 1980. A member of the NOLS faculty, Rob has led expeditions to Aconcagua and Denali, and headed numerous instructor seminars. He summitted Mt. Everest as a member of the 1994 Sagarmatha Environmental Expedition and has climbed on K2 and Gasherbrum II. An avid backcountry skier, Rob calls the northern Rockies his home and is co-director of Jackson Hole Mountain Guides.

Don Sharaf co-wrote the section on avalanche in chapter 2. He has been an instructor with NOLS since 1988 and until recently served as the school's winter coordinator.

John McMullen has written, illustrated, and designed several sports-related books. He uses his twenty years of climbing experience, which includes numerous first ascents in Colorado and Arizona, when creating technical illustrations of the sport. John is now the art director at *Climbing* magazine.

Contents

Acknowledgments

This book could not have been written without the support of the National Outdoor Leadership School.

I thank the Board of Trustees and the school's administration for realizing the book's importance and for giving me the freedom to complete it.

Many NOLS instructors and staff gave me advice and valuable critique. Thanks to Sue Miller, Greg Collins, Aileen Brew, Jim Ferguson, Tony Jewell, Liz Touhy, Georgie Stanley, Rob Hess, Molly Absolon, Tod Schimelpfenig, Jim Ratz, Debbie Derbish, Rich Brame, Patrick Clark, John Gookin, and Andy Tyson. Thanks also to all the NOLS mountaineering instructors, because what is in this book comes from all of us.

Without John McMullen's drawings, this book would be twice as long and not nearly as useful. Thanks as well to Ann Austin for her illustrations and to Lon Riesberg for his cover photo. Special thanks to Tom Hargis and Jim Ferguson for reading drafts of the second edition.

My editors, Mark Allison at Stackpole Books, and Tom Reed at NOLS gave each page the hard scrutiny it needed.

My partners at Jackson Hole Mountain Guides, Jim Ratz and Kathryn and Rob Hess, were essential to the successful completion of the second edition.

Most of all, I thank the people for whom this book is written: the students. It is the students who challenge us to strive for excellence, who keep us inspired, and who will carry our message forward.

Phil Powers
February 2000

Introduction

NOLS mountaineering courses offer the aspiring mountaineer a combination of skills, decision-making and leadership experience, and conservation philosophy. This tradition has value for those who do not have the opportunity to benefit from our expeditions, and we hope to convey some of it here in a brief text you can carry with you into the mountains.

This field text is written for NOLS mountaineering course participants and other aspiring wilderness mountaineers. It is not a substitute for professional instruction, an experienced mentor, or time in the wilderness.

THE MUST KNOWS AND THE SCOPE OF THE TEXT

NOLS founder Paul Petzoldt used the term "must know" to describe any information or knowledge fundamental to an activity. This book is a collection of must knows for wilderness mountaineering. When it comes time for you to make a decision in the mountains, you will have a fuller understanding of available options and solutions.

Many of the must knows that are prerequisites to safe wilderness mountaineering are not in this text. Camping skills are easily as important as the mountaineering information found in these pages. The key to climbing Denali, North America's highest mountain, is impeccable camping. Mountaineering decisions depend on the ability to sense and interpret data quickly, analyze potential risks, and decide upon and take appropriate action.

Warm, fed, hydrated, and acclimatized climbers are safer and more successful.

Basic backcountry travel and navigation skills are other must knows not covered in this text. The book offers insight into moving over difficult terrain, negotiating glaciers, and avoiding various mountain hazards; it does not include cross-country navigation, topographic map reading, compass use, or the intricacies of getting from the trailhead to the mountains. I encourage you to read *NOLS Wilderness Guide,* by Mark Harvey, for a comprehensive introduction to camping and traveling skills.

Think carefully about everything you do on land. A commitment to reduce impact on the backcountry must be among the goals of any wilderness expedition. The final chapter, "Style and Ethics," is devoted to wild-land ethics for the mountaineer.

Finally, the wilderness is remote from medical facilities. Backcountry climbers need wilderness first-aid training.

Each NOLS mountaineering course is unique, varying in location, terrain, weather, navigation problems, and expedition members. The order of topics in this book follows the progression of climbing instruction in an ideal course. Such a course would introduce skills from glacier navigation to steep rock climbing.

PRACTICE AND PREPARATION

Mountaineers often say that "speed is safety." It would be more appropriate to say that a mountaineer must make decisions and accomplish tasks efficiently. There are always time limits: Snow conditions change, weather threatens, and night is always on the way unless it's June in the Alaska Range. Increased efficiency and speed come only through practice. Practice should take place in a safe environment prior to challenging yourself in wild terrain.

Ultimately your skills should become second nature. Mountaineering cannot be learned without the rope and the rock or ice right there in front of you. As with riding a bicycle, you won't learn until you actually get on the thing and try. Some day, tired from a long adventure, with a descent yet to do, you will be very glad of skills learned through long practice.

Approach mountaineering in the wilderness at your own pace, with respect and patience. Master one technique before going on to others. Skills build on one another; most complex activities demand a mastery of the basics. These skills will become your "bag of tricks," which should include everything from climbing movement techniques and a knowledge of rope systems to how to analyze avalanche hazards. You will be adding more tricks to your bag throughout your life as a mountaineer.

THE ROLE OF EXPERIENCE

Safe, enjoyable mountaineering depends most on what is inside each of us. Our values and reasons for climbing, our frame of mind, and the decisions we make are far more operative in creating the mountaineering experience than are the specific skills and equipment.

A mountaineer's most important tools—judgment, decision-making skills, and what some call mountain sense—are also the hardest to learn. They develop with experience, preferably guided by a mentor or teacher, in the mountain environment. In *The Mont Blanc Massif* (London: Oxford University Press, 1974), French climbing technician and teacher Gaston Rebuffat wrote, "I wish all alpinists a big brother, a man to inspire love and respect, to keep an eye on you roping up, to take an almost tender care of you while introducing you to that tough and arduous life." Your teachers should include Rebuffat's "big brother" or "sister."

Instructor Tom Walter gave this advice on learning about mountaineering: "The way to gain important experience, and hence, develop judgment, is through a constant 'turning outward,' an incessant process of awareness of the environment around you."

NOLS teaches mountaineering on month-long expeditions. The weather, the terrain, and the remoteness do most of the teaching. Our goal is to help students become self-reliant by providing them with both the knowledge to make the right decisions at the right time and the ability to remain comfortable and healthy under any conditions, for any duration.

Do not let the amount of learning ahead or your lack of experience daunt you. If you want to climb the wild, high peaks, you will.

1

Wilderness Mountaineering

Until one is committed, there is hesitancy, a chance to draw back, always ineffectiveness. Concerning all acts of initiative (and creation), there is one elementary truth, the ignorance of which kills countless ideas and splendid plans: that the moment one definitely commits oneself, then Providence moves too. All sorts of things occur to help one that would never have otherwise occurred. A whole stream of events issue from that decision, raising in one's favor all manner of unforeseen incidents and meetings and material assistance, which no man could have dreamt would have come his way if he was still doing his thing. I have learned a deep respect for one of Goethe's couplets: "Whatever you can do or dream you can, begin it. Boldness has genius, power and magic in it."
—William H. Murray,
The Scottish Himalayan Expedition *(1951)*

The great explorer Eric Shipton wrote that "mountain climbing has its roots in mountain exploration." People toiling with heavy loads over high passes, shepherds with their herds in alpine summer pasture—these were the first mountain travelers. Remote backcountry travel is the heart and historic soul of mountaineering. Concerns for the style of an ascent and its level of difficulty are modern additions.

The pursuit of mountain summits is embedded deeply in many cultures. Incas reached high Andean peaks, Shoshone tribesmen traveled high into the Wind Rivers on vision quests, and Moses went to the mountain in search of guidance. The modern, summit-oriented pastime began in Europe. By the time Mont Blanc was climbed in 1786, Europe was already populated and hardly wild. Ascents in the Alps were one- or two-day climbs made with guides. Today people commonly ride trams rather than hike up tedious approaches. The European experience, which was the foundation of the technical development of modern mountaineering, is often not as remote as on most other continents.

Elsewhere, mountains might be deep in the wilderness, invisible from the road and miles from cell phone coverage. Reaching distant, untamed summits requires a comprehensive understanding of the environment and all manners of mountain travel. This is the case in much of North America. Ascents in the Alaska, Chugach, or Saint Elias Range may take weeks. In the Wind River Range of Wyoming, climbers travel many miles before gaining a view of their objectives. Parts of Asia's and all of Antarctica's summits are even more remote.

Expeditions of this scale require that mountaineers be capable campers and self-sufficient travelers, practiced at sustaining a comfortable life in the wilderness. This sort of mountaineering, grounded in mountain travel and expeditioning, has been taught by NOLS since 1965.

Expeditioners in the remote wilderness leave most of the crutches and aids of the modern world behind and rely on no one but themselves. The team members become cook, doctor, navigator, rescuer, friend, competitor, and companion. The rewards, from physical health to feelings of real freedom and independence and, some would argue, opened doors of perception, are reserved for those who spend the time and energy traveling far into the wild. As Walt Whitman wrote in *Leaves of Grass*, "Now I see the secret of the making of the best persons. It is to grow in the open air, and to eat and sleep with the earth."

A NOTE ON WILDERNESS

Wilderness can mean many things. It has become a legal term developed from an American consciousness that valued remote alpine summits, lakes, and forests. Our first wilderness predated the Wilderness Act of 1964 and much of it became national parks. Some of the earliest places we preserved—the Grand Tetons, Yosemite, Mount Rainier, the North Cascades, and Denali—are classic mountain terrain. Our idea of wilderness worth preserving is still tied to the cirques, tarns, and peaks of the American West.

In the United States, government-designated wilderness is a roadless area in which motorized travel is prohibited, "where the earth and its community of life are untrammeled by man, where man himself is a visitor who does not remain" (section 2[c], Wilderness Act of 1964). The wilderness I refer to in this book has a more traditional definition: the wild, natural world remote from the aids and safety nets on which so many of us rely each day of our lives.

Such places are vanishing quickly. On clear, windless days at one of earth's wildest spots—the upper flanks of Alaska's Denali at 20,320 feet—cellular phone calls and air-assisted rescues have become common. On other days, when storms pin helicopters and rescue rangers down, it remains as forbiddingly wild as ever.

Only 4.6 percent of America's land is designated as the National Wilderness Preservation System. This land is managed by the National Park Service, U.S. Forest Service, Bureau of Land Management, and U.S. Fish and Wildlife Service. Fully 60 percent of this land is found in Alaska. Many American wilderness areas have been loved to death by excessive visitation and poor camping and traveling practices. Roads and support systems of all kinds creep ever deeper into the Himalaya. Antarctica has become the new destination for hundreds of climbers and trekkers.

Fortunately, we can still experience remote wilderness. The only requirements are the skills and understanding to venture there safely, confidently, and with a minimum amount of impact upon the land.

THE ELEMENTS OF MOUNTAINEERING

Some important underlying themes in mountaineering are worth an early mention—commitment, caution, leadership, teamwork, and ethics.

COMMITMENT

Mountaineering requires a subtle mix of commitment and caution, even more so if you seek summits in remote, wild lands. Without a certain commitment, many obstacles, both small and large, keep the finest dreams from becoming reality.

CAUTION

Read climbing magazines and journals for stories of modern climbers on extraordinarily difficult routes, soloing the highest peaks and taking some very big risks. In "The Art of Climbing Down Gracefully," Tom Patey wrote, "Modern climbing is becoming fiercely competitive. Every year marks the fall of another Last Great Problem, or yet another Last Great Problem Climber. Amid this seething anthill, one must not overlook the importance of Staying Alive" (*Mountain* 16, 1971).

Every activity entails risk. Mountaineering, especially in remote locales, is dangerous and demands caution at all times. Mountaineers must ask, "What could possibly go wrong? What are the risks, and how can they be reduced?"

You can identify risk through constant awareness and assessment. Mountaineers must know their own abilities and understand the hazards of the mountain environment (see chapter 2). A prudent mountaineer foresees the consequences of every action. Caution and safety depend on your knowledge of yourself, of your partners, and of the mountain environment.

LEADERSHIP

Leadership is simple in practice. It begins with the individual. Leadership is the willingness to state an opinion, the motivation to commit to a project, and the ability to make difficult choices. It is only through each member's self-leadership that mountaineering parties can come to effective group decisions.

You must know and be honest about your own abilities and limitations. You must decide to retreat from a much-desired objective if you find it too difficult or risky. No one but you will light the stove at 4:00 A.M. to cook breakfast, and only you will get yourself out into the wild. Above all, lead yourself: speak, act, do. Leadership is well-timed, appropriate action.

TEAMWORK

Except for those who enjoy climbing alone, human interactions are a major component of any mountaineering expedition. Teamwork can be defined most simply as the effect you have on your companions; the effect can be positive or negative, motivating or distracting. Poor teamwork has been cited as a factor in many undesired mountaineering events.

Misfortunes of all kinds—from loss of life to disappointments such as not reaching goals or summitting but not enjoying the experience—have been linked to poor expedition relations. Expeditions have ground to a halt as the selfish or unthinking behavior of members takes its toll on the ability of the group to function. "Return having gained your summit, but without the good camaraderie of your companions, and what have you gained?" asks pioneer Himalayan climber Dr. Charles Houston.

There are many facets to good behavior on an expedition. Assume a full share of responsibility. Communicate your own condition to partners clearly and honestly. Simply being bearable to live with in a cramped tent during a multiday storm may be the most challenging and yet essential behavior for the mountaineer.

ETHICS

There was a time when mountaineers were the caretakers of their playgrounds and worshiped the wilderness with their care. Today, however, the mountaineer presents a threat to wild places. Himalayan expeditions leave garbage piles in otherwise pristine spots. Many ranges lost their wildness yesterday, and users must make every effort to preserve what remains for tomorrow.

For the wilderness mountaineer, Leave No Trace ethics are critical to the preservation of the land and the activity. Kind treatment of the land is inextricably tied to the future of wilderness mountaineering.

Ethics also limit the wilderness mountaineer's use of unfair technology to conquer every piece of rock, ice, and snow. Considerations for style and ethics preserve the impossible and the undoable as dreams for the future.

THE NOLS PRIORITIES

NOLS teaches that one should plan expeditions and base judgments on three priorities: safety of the individual, maintenance of the equipment, and preservation of the environment. Safety of the individual is obviously paramount.

Our concern for the equipment is really just a restatement of the other two priorities. Without equipment in good repair, you may not be able to avoid harm to yourself, your partners, or the environment. The preservation of the environment is central to the NOLS mission. The expeditioner must approach each day as if he or she were going to travel on forever across the landscape in a sustainable manner that allows the wilderness to thrive.

CLIMBING AS A LIFESTYLE AND AS A LIFELONG PURSUIT

If a yearning for the high peaks grabs your soul, there may be little you can do to resist. Mountaineering can be a lifelong endeavor, but in order to enjoy it for years to come, you must make safety a priority each time you go out.

There is a common jingle among mountaineers:

> *There are bold climbers,*
> *And there are old climbers,*
> *But there are no old, bold climbers.*

Old climbers, with their crazy stories, may seem to have been bold in yesteryear. I'll wager that, instead, they were good mountaineers who could take their abilities up to, but not beyond, a calculated edge of risk. Of course, some were just darn lucky.

As your experience begins to add up, the wilderness and the mountains will begin to come home with you. You'll think about the mountains and eat a little better, so when you next go there you'll have a little more spring in your step. You'll want to train a bit so that you can accomplish more in a week-long trip. You'll overcome obstacles and reach heights you never thought you could, returning stronger and more confident. You'll breathe a bit of good clean air, burn a few more calories than usual, and raise your heart rate. You'll decide what sort of climbing you like and the kinds of places you like to visit, and you'll develop a climbing style that expresses your personality. But whatever forms of mountaineering you pursue, you just might find that it changes your life and, most important, that the deep wilderness speaks to you.

2

Mountain Hazards

That human beings live best by living in and studying the wild is not a new idea; it is probably Pleistocene. Before the Neolithic, human beings were always living and traveling and using the lands we now call wilderness. . . . It is a tradition we need to rediscover.

—Jack Turner

Remote wilderness mountaineering demands self-reliance. There are no safety nets. Every decision has direct bearing on the comfort and success, perhaps even the survival, of your party. Far from the trailhead, climbers must camp, navigate, and dodge an environmental barrage. Mountaineering here is in its purest, least forgiving, and for many its most rewarding form. The environment deserves careful study. Its lessons may be harsh for those who have not done their homework. High peaks reward preparedness and sound camping but punish seemingly innocuous mistakes. An ill-pitched tent blows down, poorly fed climbers face hypothermia, and inefficiency may mean a night out in the cold. These are some of the risks presented by travel in remote terrain that sneak up on the unaware.

Though risk in mountaineering cannot be reduced to pure science and can never be mitigated completely, it may help to assess risk by using a simple relationship:

risk = the likelihood of an event × the consequences of that event

Using a familiar example, let's test the relationship. Bicycling up to any small-town stop sign, the cyclist confronts a certain risk. The consequences of being hit by a car while riding one's bike are dire. If the cyclist stops at the sign, checks for traffic, and then proceeds with caution, she reduces the likelihood of being hit. Using caution, the cyclist can reduce the risk to an acceptable level. If, instead, the cyclist runs the stop sign, she increases the likelihood of being hit and raises the risk to an unacceptable level. A situation in which the likelihood of an event varies but the consequences are always minor would have low risk.

Accidents are usually complicated and can rarely be blamed on a single cause. Often they result from a combination of different factors and are traceable to decisions that seemed unimportant when made. Thoroughly consider every decision you make, right down to what you have for breakfast.

In the mountains, hazards are not marked by stop signs; you must learn to identify them. We divide mountain hazards into two major categories: objective and subjective.

OBJECTIVE HAZARDS

Rockfall, avalanche, and unexpected weather are among the ongoing processes that shape the mountain world. Though mountain travelers can trigger many of these events, objective hazards are largely out of human control, and mountaineers must be proficient at recognizing them. Traveling in hazardous terrain demands that we be attentive to the route, the level of hazard, and how we move.

FALLING ROCK AND ICE

Climbing up the first pitches of the Nose of El Capitan, my partner and I became concerned when a party above us dislodged some rocks. Within a few more minutes a rather large boulder screamed by and a guide book fluttered down. Rather than spend the next days below such a proven hazard, we chose to retreat.

—Tony Jewell, Yosemite, 1986

Falling rock, ice, and objects are the third-leading cause of accidents in North American mountaineering, behind falls on rock and falls on snow or ice. (From *Accidents in North American Mountaineering.* New York: American Alpine Club, 1998.) Ice, rock, carabiners, and guidebooks all can rain down on us. We prevent the falling carabiner and guidebook by taking care not to drop them. We also must know how to protect ourselves from falling rock and ice.

Traveling through various mountain ranges, you will discover that avoiding falling rock and ice is grounded in a basic knowledge of the natural world. The geology, the climate, and the diurnal cycle of the sun all contribute to the likelihood of falling rock and ice. Route finding is easier and travel is safer when you understand what is really beneath your feet or hanging on the cliffs above your head.

You do not have to be a geologist to take note of general rock quality. Climbers who have spent much time in the mountains develop an intimate knowledge of the rock they encounter. Some know it only by layperson's terms: hard rock, soft rock, friable rock, and "antiseptic granite." Others enjoy the science and speak of quartzite, diabase, and grain size. Regardless of the language you choose, look closely at the rock and learn from it.

Note piles of rubble fallen from cliffs above. Newly fallen rocks show obvious scarring, sharp edges, and often brighter colors, while rubble from past events is dull, gray, rounded, covered by lichens and surrounded by soil development. Touch the rock and feel whether it is solid or friable. My own knowledge of geology is basic, but I take pleasure in using it to decipher the geologic history of the places I visit. It helps me understand rockfall as a hazard, and it's interesting.

The earth consists of a crust of hard rock floating on a dense mantle. Igneous rock is formed when magma in the earth's mantle cools. The result is a generally very solid and dense rock that, when uncovered by erosion, offers some of the best climbing. Some common igneous rocks are granite and diorite.

If any rock type is heated again, usually by the application of great pressure, the chemically changed result is called metamorphic rock. Metamorphic rocks, such as schist, slate, gneiss, and quartzite, are often banded and tend to fracture more easily than igneous rocks. Metamorphic and igneous rocks form the traditional playgrounds of the world's high mountain ranges.

Igneous and metamorphic rocks are thrust up by the gnashing together of huge plates of crust circulated by movement in the mantle. Once exposed to the atmosphere, these rocks begin to weather and break down. Smaller particles are eroded and deposited elsewhere. This material, when deposited in layers on valley bottoms or ocean floors, is compressed into sedimentary rock. Sedimentary rocks, such as limestone and sandstone, are softer and generally more breakable than igneous and metamorphic rocks.

If the mountains were thrust tall and left untouched by the forces of nature, we'd have some mighty high mountains to climb and less rockfall hazard. But as they rise, mountains are weathered away. As John McPhee writes in *Rising from the Plains* (New York: Farrar, Straus & Giroux, 1987), "In the contest between erosion and orogeny [mountain formation], erosion never loses." Huge rock peaks are broken down into smaller pieces by forces of weathering: Wind, water, freeze and thaw, acids from plant life, and even the passage of animals contribute to the disintegration. These smaller pieces are then transported downslope by forces of erosion and mass wasting. Most forms of erosion—water, glacier, avalanche, soil creep—happen at a rate in proportion to slope angle: The steeper the slope, the more and the faster material moves. On flat surfaces, like the high peneplains of the Wind Rivers, weathered material just sits in place.

Climate—the large-scale atmospheric changes that come with the seasons—influences weathering and the annual cycle of snow and ice. Local climatic conditions, taken together with rock type and slope angle, provide a general, but important, group of clues to help predict the potential for falling ice and rock. Climate and weather are significant factors in loosening rocks and ice.

Look around and ask some questions. Are even intrusive igneous rocks highly fractured and loose? Is ice forming every night, prying rocks apart as it expands, then melting every day, sending them tumbling downslope? Weather and climate can cause similar rock types to have quite different levels of stability.

For example, the rock high in the northern Wind River Range is much more broken and dangerous than that in Yosemite, because thousands of years of freeze-thaw activity has loosened the Wind River granite, while the rock in Yosemite has weathered slowly in a temperate climate since the glaciers receded.

Annual climatic cycles play seasonal roles in the level of hazard. As ice and snow melt back in the spring, rocks loosened during the winter tumble and pieces of ice fall. Droughts free rocks that have been kept from falling for years by ice, making the mountains virtual shooting galleries.

On a narrower time frame, diurnal cycles and slope aspect are very important to route choice and timing. Daily thaws melt ice and loosen rocks, causing them to fall at different times according to the slope's aspect—the direction it faces. In the Northern Hemisphere, east faces thaw first, then south, and then west at the end of the day. Rain can undermine the integrity of many types of sedimentary rocks or quickly change the condition of a snow slope. Local weather conditions should influence your route choice. The key is to watch the weather's effects and use your observations to predict hazards and choose a safe route. It is not uncommon for a mountaineering party to watch a route for a day or even over a week in an effort to determine its hazards.

Other forms of weathering have more subtle effects. Plants may seem to stabilize a slope, but their roots actually may be undermining the rock on which the slope is anchored. Chemical weathering may have rotted granite that appears solid.

Avoiding Falling Rock and Ice

Environmental factors influence rockfall and icefall in an ongoing process. Objects fall without warning. Therefore, identify and avoid the paths that the rocks will most likely take and the times they will most likely fall. Also, avoid gullies and couloirs (steep mountainside gorges)—especially those fed by bowls, or tributary gullies—with signs of rockfall at the base. Stay on ridges as much as possible. Be especially aware of steep-sided couloirs and other situations that might cause rock or ice to ricochet into protected spots.

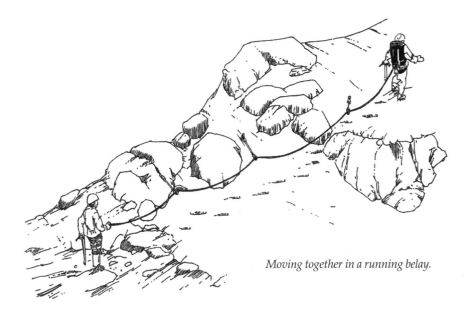

Moving together in a running belay.

Time your travel to coincide with periods of decreased hazard intensity. Travel when ice is still frozen and rocks are held in place or when meltwater is least active. Do not climb routes, especially couloirs, until they are in good condition. Observe routes before traveling them, checking to see if there is any diurnal pattern to the hazard, and then move quickly during the lulls. It is often wise to watch a route for at least twenty-four hours before your attempt.

Finally, plan routes carefully so you can move quickly between protected spots. It may be better to cross a danger zone by its shortest distance, even though this may add to the length of your overall route.

Preventing Objects From Falling

You have the power to control a significant percentage of falling rock and ice. Carelessness and insufficient knowledge are your worst enemies. Reinhold Messner, writing in *The Armchair Mountaineer,* went so far as to suggest that we could even influence spontaneous objective hazards:

I am not saying that a man's will can stop rocks breaking away or hinder the passage of avalanches—only that a man who is in contact with himself and his surroundings is unlikely to find himself in their path. I would stick my neck out and suggest that the mentally well-adjusted climber won't perish on a mountain—or, put another way, every mountain accident has its human ingredient.

Every accident does have a human ingredient—its subjective hazard—which often includes a lack of attentiveness to the problems and dangers at hand. Distraction and the inability to fully understand the information nature offers increases risk, and people often cause rockfall and icefall. You can take steps to actively prevent such hazards using the following techniques:

1. Test holds and ice placements. Climb with even weight distribution, and push holds into the mountain rather than down its slope. If rock or ice comes loose, try to replace it or direct it away from other members of the group.

2. Take breaks, place belays, and gather your party in sheltered locales. Falling rock and ice ricochet at astounding angles, so taking shelter under overhangs is safer than just being out of the direct fall-line.

3. Know when you can relax and take advantage of mental rest; otherwise, stay alert.

4. When moving up loose rock, keep groups in a tight line, one person right after another, so dislodged rocks don't gain momentum. If possible, move en echelon. When you encounter short sections of hazard, pass through them one climber at a time, while others wait, protected.

5. Be creative and efficient with rope management: Place gear to keep the rope from dislodging loose rocks and to direct followers to the safest line. Keep rope neat and well protected from falling objects. Coil and carry ropes when they are not needed in a safety system.

6. When setting top ropes, especially at unfrequented sites, rappel and clean loose rock from the routes before climbing. Keep the rope in butterflies, draped over the rope

immediately above the rappel device, or loosely stacked in a bag, and pay it out as you descend; rope thrown to the ground might be damaged by dislodged rocks.

Reacting To Falling Objects

The warning signal for any falling object is *"Rock!"* A film of an early NOLS course shows Paul Petzoldt yelling, *"Rock!"* and then winging something down at his students. Lobbing projectiles at others is outside what most consider acceptable teaching techniques, but Petzoldt's unorthodox technique taught students to stay out of the rock fall zone or become adept at hustling to safety. Use the following techniques to keep from being injured by falling rock and ice:

1. When in a danger zone or on steep terrain, wear a helmet. Ice climbs are especially hazardous, because the ax and crampon placements can dislodge a great deal of ice.
2. If ice, rock, carabiners, water bottles, or any other objects fall or are about to fall, everybody who notices should loudly yell, *"Rock!"* Others should repeat this signal to ensure that all in the vicinity hear.
3. When in a danger zone, be prepared to react to the signal *"Rock!"* with one of the following techniques:
   a. If near the base of the cliff, press up close against the steepest or most overhanging section, and hide under your helmet.
   b. If belaying, hide under your helmet and move your brake hand to brake position.
   c. If not near the base of the cliff, move quickly to a sheltered spot, such as behind a tree or boulder, or well away from the base of the cliff.
4. Rarely, when an object is falling from a great distance or rolling slowly, it is appropriate to look up and attempt to predict its path.

The above reactions must be preconditioned. Constantly consider the risk and preplan the best escape. Train yourself to always be ready. Preventing and avoiding falling ice and rock are too big a task for anything but your fullest attention. Your team's safety depends on it.

BOULDERS AND TALUS

Rocks underneath your feet can also be a hazard. Boulders and talus are often treacherous, especially when the mountain traveler is carrying a heavy pack or is tired after a long climb.

Talus and boulders on a slope are usually sorted by size. Larger rocks tumble to the bottom; medium-size rocks stabilize in the middle; and small rocks and pebbles lie loosely near the top. These slopes are examples of erosion in progress, and any rock may be ready to roll under the feet of an unwary hiker. Generally, the best routes are on the medium-size rocks halfway up the slope. The giant boulders near the bottom are difficult to negotiate, and the small, loose rocks higher up slide and impede travel.

The stability of a boulder field depends largely on its age. Newly deposited boulders are unpredictable, and a turned ankle or broken leg may be the consequence of crossing a young, unstable boulder field with abandon. Older depositions, marked by soil accumulation and large lichens on the rocks, are more stable and less likely to roll under your feet; here you can move much faster.

On all boulder fields, it is best to step on the centers of rocks to keep them from rolling under your feet. Avoid stepping down between boulders. This slows travel, and if your feet land on the sides of rocks, the rocks may roll over onto legs or feet.

SWIFT WATER

When I was NOLS chief mountaineering instructor, I was asked what were some of the most significant hazards that mountaineers face. River crossings immediately came to mind. On two of NOLS's most advanced mountaineering courses at that time, the Denali expedition and the Aconcagua expedition, river crossings were clearly among the most dangerous events. Could it be that the greatest mountain hazards are found in the valleys?

Brooks and streams are easily negotiated; you often can step across them or walk across on boulders. But there is still a certain hazard. Take precautions even in simple river crossings. Offer one another a hand, and use an ice ax or stick to aid your balance. If you choose to cross on a log or via boulders, consider not only whether you can cross but also what might happen if you fall in. When logs or boulders are slimy or icy, try spreading sand on them. Consider trying to cross without a pack first, just to scout the site.

Many larger rivers are impossible to cross without the aid of a bridge or a boat. It is important to do research before the expedition in order to learn what is out there and if the route you've selected is feasible.

The class of in-between rivers presents the greatest difficulty. They are small enough that you can cross them but too large to simply hop across on boulders or logs. These rivers must be treated with respect, and crossing them takes time.

Because most mountain rivers are fed by snowmelt, their levels fluctuate with the time of day and amount of sunshine on distant snowfields and glaciers. A river generally will be at its lowest level in the morning. Some rivers can be crossed only at these low ebbs in their diurnal cycle. Hard and prolonged rainfall can also have a significant effect, raising river levels as much as one foot in thirty minutes and stranding half a group on one side.

When in doubt, scout! First and foremost, take some time to look upstream and down for the easiest crossings. There may be a good place to cross, even a bridge, just out of view. For large and dangerous rivers, it may be worth scouting a mile or two in each direction to find a likely crossing. When scouting a river, one or two people can go upstream and one or two down. Set a time to reconvene that allows you to scout well. Time limits serve as "freak times": Teammates know not to "freak" and begin a search until their partners are truly late.

Read the water to find the best crossing. Look for a widening of the river where the current has slowed and the river is shallower. With luck you will be able to see the bottom and gauge its depth. In glacial runoffs, the bottom is obscured by the milky sediments carried in the water, so test the depth with an ice ax or long pole. If moving water is so deep it hits the torso, crossings are very difficult or impossible. Velocity is often a good indicator of water depth. Faster water forced into a narrow channel may result in surprising depth. Avoid free-flowing channels of fast water.

Eddies are areas of lower water velocity that occur below river obstacles such as large rocks, logs, or encroaching banks. Sometimes, especially in larger crossings, it is advantageous to move from eddy to eddy, spending as little time as possible in the main current.

Tributaries offer the solution to many river-crossing problems. If a river is too large to cross safely, consider traveling upstream until it divides into smaller tributaries. Glacial rivers often can be crossed as a series of tributaries broken by gravel bars. Sometimes the gravel bars themselves are underwater but still offer shallow, stable respites after deeper channels.

Crossing Methods

Once a spot is chosen, you must decide on a crossing method. In shallow water, many veteran mountaineers walk quickly so their gaiters keep their socks dry. This method is known affectionately as the Mississippi high-step. In slightly deeper water, people might step across from boulder to boulder. Consider having the more adroit rockhoppers shuttle packs. In even deeper water, consider wading in boots. Think twice about wading in light sneakers or bare feet. It is easy to turn an ankle or cut a foot. The protection boots provide on land is even more important in a cold mountain river. If wading in boots, take your socks off and keep them dry.

In deep, fast water, you'll need acquired expertise to keep from being swept away. Fast water not only pushes you around, but it moves the riverbottom as well. Avoid crossings where you hear the sound of rocks crashing into one another on the bottom.

Get good at "hairy" crossings by practicing on a warm day with serious waters that push your limits. Try team crossings, but also try going alone; on your next expedition, you may be the only one who can assess whether something is crossable. Use a long, stout stick to create a tripod effect. Face upstream. Shuffle across the stream with your eyes focused on the bank, since star-

Spotters in place with one person crossing.

ing at riverbottoms or the moving surface can be dizzying. Keep moving. If you stand still for long, you'll be riding those tumbling stones. With practice, most people can cross crotch-deep swift water. Without practice, most people wipe out in that same situation. Some methods worth trying include the following:

- Shuffle across one at a time, using others as spotters. Use a long, stout stick as a third point of balance.
- *The eddy-line crossing.* Cross in lines, each person downstream from the next and holding on to the person in front. The upstream person, who should be the strongest river crosser, produces an eddy and reduces the current hitting those downstream. Because of the eddy produced by the head of the line and the stability added by people supporting from behind, this is an excellent method in deep water.
- *The chain crossing.* Cross in threes or fours holding hands. This method allows more proficient crossers (ends of the line) to support less proficient crossers (middle of the line). This method is generally used when the water is below the knee or when the river bottom is irregular and the group needs to weave; it is not as effective in deeper water. A variation is for team members to hold onto a long pole, rather than each other's hands. This method has proved very secure.

Before making a difficult crossing, be sure all your equipment is tightly packed away. Release your pack waist belt and sternum strap for quick removal if you fall down during the crossing. Be sure spotters are well placed and ready.

If you do wipe out in deep water, get out of your pack, face downstream, and sit in the river with your feet up and forward so they will take the brunt of anything you hit. "Ferry" across to a close bank or the outside of a bend; let your arms do the swimming. A foot can easily become trapped between large boulders in fast water, so do not try to stand up until you are near the bank. Look for spotters who might hold a long stick or pile jacket out for you to grab and pull you toward the bank.

The traditional method among water experts for helping a swimmer back to the bank is to throw a rope to the swimmer. Though the use of a rope is effective for those with water-rescue training, if used improperly it can easily entangle the swimmer and make the situation worse. Therefore, spotters should reach for the swimmer with a stick or pile jacket but should not throw a rope unless trained in the technique. Spotters are the rescuers and should not endanger themselves.

Once you are out of the river, locate your pack and hope like crazy that it washes out on your side of the river. Wiping out can be a dangerous and exhausting experience; if you do, rewarm, rest, eat, and drink before continuing your journey.

WEATHER

Mountaineers need to be able to anticipate weather changes so they can prepare for them. Even the worst weather is not a hazard if you are ready for it. But weather can be dangerous when it changes unexpectedly or when a team is unprepared for the conditions. At a minimum, you should learn a few of the early signs of changing weather to help your short-term forecasting.

The following basic facts will help you understand what is happening in the atmosphere:

1. Air has mass. The more densely it is packed into a given volume, the heavier it is.
2. Cooler air molecules have less energy, move more slowly, and can be packed more tightly into a given volume. A

given volume of cool air is heavier than the same volume of warm air. Warm air, because it is lighter, will rise.

3. Warm air is moist because it has the space and energy to hold more moisture.

4. As air rises, it cools. Since cooler air cannot hold as much moisture, that moisture condenses into water droplets, causing precipitation.

5. In North America, prevailing winds, and hence most weather changes, come from the west.

You can use this information to make your next wilderness experience more comfortable. For example, being aware that cold air sinks and accumulates in low spots, you will know not to place your camp at the bottom of a valley, which is the coldest area at night.

Orographic Weather

In order to be prepared for weather changes, you need to understand orographic weather, those patterns associated with mountains. In the mountains, the mornings are often clear but clouds build up by midafternoon. Sometimes they bring thundershowers, which in the Tetons come each afternoon like clockwork. The reason for these storms is simple. Air, with a certain amount of moisture in it, moves with the prevailing winds from west to east. When air moving across the flats hits a mountain range, it is forced up and over; it cools, and the moisture condenses into clouds and rain. Cloud build-up is accelerated during the day by heat reflecting off the mountainsides, which warms the air and dries it upward.

From your perch on a belay ledge, you can watch the clouds start to form. During the approach, there may have been no clouds at all. Then there is a tiny wisp or two, and before you know it the sky is filled with small, puffy cumulus clouds, which form when air is moving vertically. They look like fair-weather clouds through the morning, but then, when you look once more, they have become towering thunderheads. When these thunderheads finally build up, usually in the midafternoon, they can result in wind, rain, and lightning. But if you recognize the patterns and plan accordingly—by getting off the high points early or retreating when storms threaten—orographic weather is of no great concern. Many mountaineers plan to summit by noon and descend by 2:00 P.M., hence the simple maxim "On by noon, off by two." This takes planning and, more important, the discipline to start your climb early and keep moving.

Another local event that can help mountaineers understand weather is the formation of lenticular clouds—lens-shaped or saucerlike clouds that sometimes form over mountain summits. These clouds indicate high winds and cold air near the mountaintop and can be a clue that, although the weather may be generally clear, conditions at the summit are nasty.

Pressure Fronts

Pressure fronts are big and hard to predict, and they bring about weather changes that last longer. There are two basic types: cool, high-pressure systems and warm, low-pressure systems. Driven by the prevailing westerly winds, the high or low shoves the existing air mass along to the east.

A high-pressure system is a mass of cooler, and therefore heavier, air. A low-pressure system is formed by warm, moist air, which is relatively lighter. Air from the highs is constantly moving toward and attempting to fill the relative vacuum of the lows. The interfaces between highs and lows are known as fronts. It is along these fronts that winds tend to blow more, because there the difference in air pressure between the high and the low is most pronounced.

Cool air—high pressure—is heavier and sinks in under the low-pressure system it displaces. As this air moves in, it forces warm, moist air higher, where it condenses into water droplets. This happens in a matter of hours and may cause brief but heavy rain and lightning. Cold fronts travel fast and don't give much warning. High winds, violent weather changes, and vertical air movement in the form of towering cumulus clouds signal the passing cold front. With them comes a mass of cooler air, which typically holds less moisture. You could say a cold front announces the arrival of pleasant weather, violently.

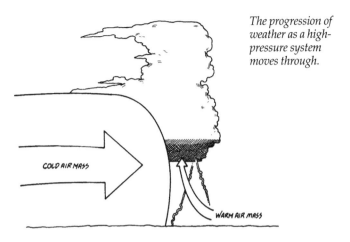

The progression of weather as a high-pressure system moves through.

COLD AIR MASS

WARM AIR MASS

Warm fronts, on the other hand, move slowly, and the change in weather they bring is not abrupt. They are characterized by the flat stratus clouds formed by air moving horizontally. The warmer air is lighter and tends to ride up over the cold air being displaced. In the early stages, air is pushed up high enough to form ice crystals when the moisture condenses. As the high-pressure system is pushed east, we experience warm, moist air in lowering stratus clouds. Warm fronts may take days to pass, and if they carry much moisture, they will drop buckets of it in the mountains.

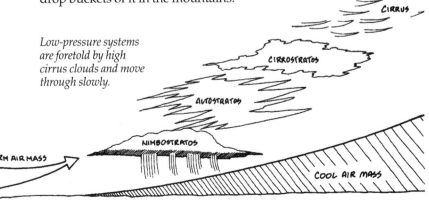

Low-pressure systems are foretold by high cirrus clouds and move through slowly.

CIRRUS

CIRROSTRATOS

AUTOSTRATOS

NIMBOSTRATOS

WARM AIR MASS

COOL AIR MASS

Early cirrus clouds, often called mackerel sky or mare's tails, are the best early-warning signs of a low-pressure system. Though there may be breaks of clear sky, ever lowering and increasing stratus clouds are a sure sign the weather is changing. These systems are usually large and slow moving. They may take days to pass.

It may help your forecasting skills to know that low-pressure systems and their winds rotate counterclockwise. The wind you feel on your face is not indicative of the direction of the larger continental winds or the movement of the pressure system. To learn where the storm center is, look to the clouds. Which direction are they coming from? Face that direction and point to your right. You are pointing at the center of the storm.

Weather is not good or bad or even a hazard in and of itself; it is only notable in relation to our expectations. *Accidents in North American Mountaineering* lists "unexpected weather" as an unsafe condition and cause of accidents. You can minimize weather as a hazard by observing the following guidelines:

1. Expect the worst. Plan your gear and trip in anticipation of the extremes for an area and time of year. Think, "What if the weather turns very nasty while we're on this route?" and have some contingencies in mind.

2. Be an effective camper and traveler so that difficult weather conditions will not wear you down or affect your judgment.

3. Know the early signs of changing weather, and adjust your plans accordingly.

4. If you expect whiteout conditions and are traveling on snow, use bamboo wands to mark your route back to camp. Placed every 100 to 200 feet, they can lead you back home in some of the worst visibility. (High on K2, we placed them 50 feet apart.)

5. Take and record a compass bearing so you can use it on your descent in case visibility deteriorates.

6. Know first aid treatment for illnesses caused by weather: heat exhaustion and heatstroke, sunburn, hypothermia, and frostbite.

LIGHTNING

Lightning is a sudden discharge of electricity or, more accurately, of electrons. When there is a significant difference in electrical potential between a cloud and the ground or another cloud, and this builds up too quickly in one place, lightning results. Quick, vertical air movement is usually the reason static electricity builds up so fast. This air movement is often associated with cold fronts or afternoon thundershowers. In the same way that shuffling your feet on a carpet builds static electricity, faster and more prolonged air movement increases lightning intensity.

The vertical air movement that causes lightning is indicated by towering cumulus clouds. As they build over the course of a storm or during daily orographic weather, be alert to the possibility of lightning. The classic thunderhead is a cumulonimbus cloud—often so high that winds blow the top of the cloud into an anvil shape.

Lightning bolts carry trillions of watts of electrical power; harnessing a few bolts could satiate some of the world's appetite for energy. We see the discharge of energy as a flash of light at the instant it occurs. The movement of superheated air causes claps of thunder, which we experience a little later. You can determine the distance between you and the hazard by the amount of time it takes for the thunder to reach your ears. Sound moves at about 1,000 feet per second at sea level, so the sound of thunder travels about 1 mile in five seconds. If lightning is only 1 mile away, you are in danger. Check several times to determine whether the storm is moving toward you or away. You may learn that it is sitting out over the plains or that it is coming quickly and you must take precautions.

There are other indications of imminent lightning. As electrical current builds up before a strike, you may hear a crackling noise or smell ozone. Hair may stand on end. Objects may take on an eerie blue glow, known as Saint Elmo's fire. It indicates the presence of static electricity and hence the possibility of a strike. If you experience any of these signs or if the thunder closely follows the strike, take immediate action, using some of the following guidelines:

- Lightning usually strikes the highest points in an area. Avoid being the highest point or standing on or near the highest point. Descend before the hazard arrives.
- Avoid places that will conduct current through the ground. Moist areas and drainages of all sizes will readily conduct the current.
- Avoid rappelling when lightning is imminent. Wet ropes can conduct current.
- Do not take refuge in shallow caves or under small over-hangs. Ground current is likely to take a "shortcut" through you to the ground below. Large, deep caves will provide protection, however.
- Insulate yourself from ground current by crouching on a pack, coiled rope, or ensolite pad.
- Keep feet close together so current is not likely to travel up one leg and down the other. Keep hands off the ground.
- Set metal objects aside. They don't actually attract the strike but might heat up or burn you via direct transmission of current.

If lightning strikes at or near your party, the energy may cause injury in several different ways:

- A direct strike may actually hit someone.
- Lightning might be deflected off an object and strike some-one nearby.
- A person may receive a direct transmission of electricity by being in contact with an object that is struck.
- A person may come in contact with ground current as elec-tricity dissipates from an object that has been struck.
- Lightning superheats the air through which it travels. This produces a shock wave that can hit people and can cause injury.

Any team traveling into the backcountry should be well versed in wilderness first aid, including the treatment of electrical burns that may be caused by lightning. Direct strikes are rare, but when they do occur, the resulting injuries may be internal and difficult to detect. The nervous system is easily damaged by electricity; cardiac arrest, respiratory failure, and damage to the brain or spinal cord may occur. Persons who are not breathing or lack a pulse should be given artificial respiration or CPR immediately.

Most people are injured by ground or splash currents. These follow lines of moisture through the body and inflict electrical burns in distinct patterns that may be either circular or linear. Showers of electrons may leave feathery burns on the skin's surface. In addition to burns, lightning victims may suffer other injuries from both the shock wave and the electrical current. It is imperative that rescuers conduct a thorough secondary survey.

See chapter 4, "Burns and Lightning Injuries," in *NOLS Wilderness First Aid* for more information.

HIGH ALTITUDE

The weight of air above us compresses molecules at sea level. We are adapted to breathing the denser air that exists at altitudes where we live. Higher, in the mountains, the air is less dense, and each breath brings fewer molecules of oxygen into the lungs. Air at high altitude is also under less pressure and is not forced as readily from the lungs into the bloodstream. The resulting hazard for the mountaineer is hypoxia, or lack of oxygen.

People begin to feel the symptoms of hypoxia at various elevations beginning about 8,000 feet above sea level. Air pressure decreases geometrically as altitude increases, so the effects of hypoxia increase disproportionately as one climbs higher. Problems adjusting to altitude sneak up on the unaware and can be a serious and possibly fatal hazard.

Symptoms of hypoxia may be mild but usually have a quick or acute onset. Decreased respirations during sleep may speed their onset. "Feeling the altitude" is known to the medical profession as acute mountain sickness (AMS). Symptoms include headache, shortness of breath, dehydration, nausea, decreased urine output, and in some cases, dizziness. AMS is not a life-threatening illness but indicates that the individual may not be acclimatizing well.

People can acclimatize to higher elevations if their bodies are given adequate time. Above 8,000 feet, most physicians recommend climbing at a rate of only 1,500 feet per day. This rate is based on the elevation at which one sleeps. You may gain more elevation during a day as long as you descend and sleep no more than 1,500 feet higher than the previous night. Acclimatization varies with the individual, and some climbers manage much faster rates of ascent.

Some physical adaptations begin to take effect in a matter of days; most people become well acclimatized to a new elevation within ten days. Other adaptations take many weeks. Climbers with ambitions at extreme altitudes (above 20,000 feet, for example) often reserve several weeks for acclimatization before attempting their objectives. Good hydration, conservative rates of ascent, and taking care never to become exhausted all facilitate your adjustment to high elevations.

Climbing too fast may have significant consequences. High altitude pulmonary edema (HAPE) and high altitude cerebral edema (HACE) are acute illnesses that can kill a climber quickly. With HAPE, the lungs fill with fluid and the symptoms are similar to those of pneumonia. HACE develops from pressure changes inside the skull. Fluids accumulate and cause severe headaches and the loss of judgment, motivation, balance, and even consciousness.

If you plan mountaineering expeditions to high altitudes, learn the intricacies of mountain sickness. High altitude illnesses are unpredictable, so it is important to recognize the signs and symptoms (see *NOLS Wilderness First Aid*). Schedule time to acclimatize, and know how and when to evacuate a stricken teammate. The treatment for any altitude sickness is a rapid descent to a lower elevation.

AVALANCHE

Ice avalanches can be devastating. Hanging glaciers and glacial seracs often seem to calve off unpredictably. The daily effects of sun and changing temperatures increase the likelihood of icefall. Travel when the sun is not shining on such features, and avoid being beneath them when temperatures are changing dramatically, as they do when sunshine arrives or leaves the ice. In the glaciated ranges of Alaska, mountaineers sometimes travel at night.

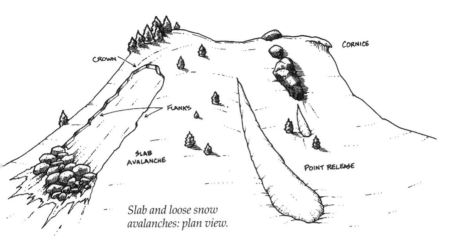

Slab and loose snow avalanches: plan view.

Climbers also avoid ice avalanches by knowing the history of a site, examining debris evidence, and maintaining a very conservative safety margin, especially when making camp. Speedy travel through avalanche-prone areas minimizes exposure time.

Snow avalanches are somewhat more predictable than ice. They come in two varieties: slab and loose snow. Slabs are layers of snow that hold together as a unit. When these cohesive layers fracture and shear, the result can be a devastating snowslide. Point release avalanches start at a single point, one snow crystal or snowball that then entrains more snow, causing the slide to grow in size as it runs downhill.

Slab Avalanches

Slab avalanches are one of the biggest hazards in the alpine environment, whether it is mid-January or late July.

Evaluating a given couloir or face that you want to climb for avalanche potential involves the interplay of four factors: terrain, snowpack, weather, and the human factor. As a mountaineer, most of your snow and ice routes will be in terrain capable of producing an avalanche. With that in mind, you need to learn what terrain will minimize your exposure to avalanche hazard and how to identify microterrain features. Learning to accurately read a snowpack takes years of experience and practice, but there

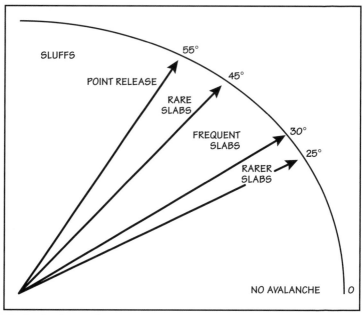

Avalanche slope angles.

are some guidelines to start with. Knowing how weather affects the snowpack is crucial to your climbing. Putting all your analyses together into a decision involves the human factor, which is the source of most mistakes. Most important, realizing that avalanches often follow the exceptions rather than the rules should throw a healthy dose of conservatism into your judgments. The information is almost always there, but our interpretations may be biased by our ambitions.

Point Release Avalanches

The most useful factor in determining the level of hazard for either sort of avalanche is the angle of the slope on which the snow sits. On flat or very low-angle slopes, the snow has no inclination to slide. On gentle slopes, only very lubricated snow will slide. These avalanches are generally wet, point release slides that move quite slowly and usually can be avoided easily. They are, however, dense and powerful. If you are caught or hit by one, it may carry you into hazardous terrain features, such as crevasses or cliffs.

The steepest slopes are also conducive to point release slides. On slopes above 55 degrees, snow does not stick well and sloughs off in frequent point release slides. The volume of snow may be small and of little consequence, but because of the steep slopes, these slides move extremely fast. A slide of this sort comes suddenly and without warning and often catches climbers in vulnerable positions.

Terrain. Angles that can produce large slab avalanches commonly lie between 30 and 45 degrees. These slab avalanches can occur on slightly lower-angle slopes when snow conditions are particularly weak or wet; they can also occur on higher-angle slopes but are generally smaller in size. Slopes that are greater than 45 degrees or have abundant wet snow at the surface can move as loose snow sluffs or point release slides. Slopes greater than 60 degrees rarely hold snow for long, but wet snowfall with high winds can often plaster rock faces with layers of new snow or rime. (Rime deposits are white, feathery formations of ice formed by wind and clouds; they build on the windward side of an object or human.) Be wary of snow and ice coming off these faces immediately following storms, particularly on the first clearing after a storm.

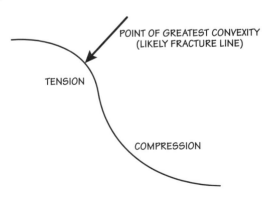

The crown fracture of a slab avalanche is most likely to occur at the point of greatest convexity in the slope.

Aspect is the direction that a slope faces. In the Northern Hemisphere, a slope facing due south will catch far more sunlight than one that faces north. Whether that is good or bad depends on many variables, including the snowpack composition.

Possibly even more significant than the amount of sunlight is the amount of wind-transported snow a slope may receive. Climbers and skiers call this process wind loading. The prevailing wind direction can be inferred from a number of clues, including the direction that cornices face, flagging on trees, and wind scouring on windward sides of mountains. In addition, the wind direction for the last snowfall can be determined by the presence of sastrugi, or wind waves, in the snow; local "fat" wind deposits or pillows; and rime on rocks and trees.

Snow is often removed from the windward side of a mountain or a ridge and then deposited on the leeward side. Prevailing winds in the midlatitudes of North America are typically from the southwest or the west, which means northeast- to east-facing slopes will typically be loaded during storms. South-central Alaska and coastal British Columbia often see southeast prevailing winds. These extra wind loads can make slopes more prone to avalanche.

Features can minimize or increase the amount of exposure to avalanches from above. Gullies or couloirs tend to funnel avalanches. When snow conditions are unstable, or when new snow is falling, these are places to avoid. Faces offer few escape routes. An important consideration when climbing a face is its shape. If it is convex or has a breakover from a lower angle to a higher angle, then that area may be under the most tension and consequently may be a likely starting point for an avalanche. Ridges often provide some degree of safety. Snow essentially flows like water as it seeks out lower elevations. If a ridge is sharp and stands away from the mountain, it will provide a much safer route than a broad, open ridge that blends into a face. Keep looking up, because a small subridge gives very little protection when there is a large avalanche track above.

Snowpack. Whether you are in the Coast Range of British Columbia in May, the Alaska Range in June, or the Tetons in January, there will likely be some degree of layering in the snowpack. Figuring out whether the bonds between the layers are strong enough to hold the snow loads above is the main question to ask yourself in the mountains. From the minute you start your climbing trip to the time you leave, observe how the snow behaves. Traveling into new and steep terrain, it is best to take a day to observe the changes in the surface snow's stability during daylight hours—a great challenge to mountaineers who have been holed up in their tents and are eager to get on their route. Observe such things as the following:

- Is sluffing occurring when the sun hits a given aspect? How much longer does it occur after the slopes first receive sunlight?
- Are avalanches running onto lower-angle slopes, and what angles are they confined to?
- How hard is the surface snow freezing at night, if at all?
- Is there any wind transport of new snow going on?
- Are there fresh mounds of avalanche debris at the bases of gullies?
- Is the new snow sliding on old snow, or on an ice layer, bedrock, or the ground?

One April on Mount Saint Elias in southeast Alaska, three days of heavy snowfall and high winds ended with a fourth day of perfect climbing weather. All morning the slopes avalanched as they came into the sun. It was like a giant sundial—first the east-facing slopes slid, then the southeast, then the south, and on into the afternoon, when the west-facing slopes ended the day's avalanche symphony.

TESTING THE SNOW

In subfreezing temperatures, you need to be concerned about a lot more than the bond of the most recent snow to the old snow beneath, as weak layers can persist far below the most recent snow interface. There are three components in a slab avalanche: a slab (cohesive unit of snow) overlying a weak layer on top of a bed surface. A bed surface is a sliding surface harder than the weak layer above it. It could be an interface with old snow, glacier ice, or the ground. Numerous tests exist to help determine snow stability in the winter, many of them involving skis or shovels. Covering them all is beyond the scope of this book, but a few tests that you should be able to do any time of the year and throughout any travel or climbing day include the shovel shear test, pole or ax probing, and stomping on the snow.

Shovel shear tests don't tell everything about the stability of the snow, but they can give an indication of where there are potentially weaker bonds between snow layers. Isolate a column of snow on all four sides by digging out the downhill side 12 inches across, 12 inches uphill on both sides, and then cutting the back as well. Using a snow saw, ice ax, or your hand (in order of efficiency and precision), cut away the snow on the sides of the column so they don't interfere with the column, then insert your shovel (or pot lid, or hand—whatever you have) behind the column—only as deep as you can go without prying or levering the column away from the back wall—and pull toward yourself. If there is a very clean or flat surface where the top layer broke away from the layers below, that is a layer to watch, especially if it came out with light pressure from the back.

A less time-consuming version of this test can be done with your hands. Isolate a small column of snow and pull on it. This takes less than twenty seconds and can give you

(continued)

TESTING THE SNOW continued

information about how the surface snow is changing on your approach to the climb or the climb itself. This can be especially helpful as you near the top of your climb and the new wind slab is becoming deeper and deeper. The more often you perform hand or shovel shears, the more information you get on how the snowpack changes over space. The superstrong snow of the lower apron of your climb may have turned into rotten mush, with a supporting crust on top, higher on the route.

Pole or ax probing is as simple a test as you can perform, but it gives you valuable information about how the snow layers are changing. If you shove your ski pole or ice ax to its full depth, do you encounter a zone of less resistance? The ease with which you can push your pole or ax into the snow can tell you whether you have a light-over-heavy layering, homogenous snowpack, or a heavy-over-light sequence, in which case warning flags should be flying.

Stomping on steep, isolated rollovers that will present no hazard to you if they do slide is a great way to get immediate feedback on how the upper snow layers are bonding to the lower ones. If you have skis on, check to see how the snow behaves when you make a switchback turn. If it breaks and slides onto your lower track, this means a slab and a weak layer are present. Shooting cracks, *whumpf* sounds, and natural avalanches are all warning signs of instability.

When digging pits, it is important to choose sites that are safe—places that won't avalanche or where the consequences would be minimal—and that are representative of the slope. They should have a similar angle, aspect, and elevation to what you want to climb or descend. Keep in mind that conditions can change as you move across, up, or down the slope. Snow observations should be an ongoing process; a pit is just one piece of the big picture.

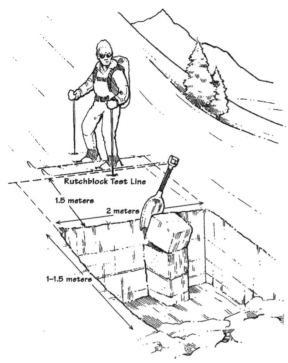

Rutchblock Test Line

1.5 meters

2 meters

1–1.5 meters

Shown here are both the column for a shovel shear test and the cuts made above the pit for the more accurate predictor, the rutchblock test. In the rutchblock test, performed after the shear test column is removed, an average-size skier approaches the cut-out block above the pit. The lower the score, the greater the hazard:

R1: Block fractures as skier approaches.
R2: Block fractures as skier steps onto it.
R3: Block fractures when skier flexes knees.
R4: Block fractures when skier jumps.
R5: Block fractures on second jump.
R6: Block fractures when skier moves to mid-block and performs up to 3 jumps.
R7: No failure.

Weather. If snowpack is the major factor determining current snow stability, then weather is the forecasting factor. The wind, sun, temperature, and rainfall may all have a significant impact on the snow's stability for the time ahead on the climb.

Loose snow can be moved by wind even at moderate speeds (greater than 15 miles per hour). Whether leeward slopes will pick up significant amounts of wind-transported snow depends on the depth of snow that can be moved, the strength and duration of the wind, and the area that is scoured. High winds can remove all available snow—even heavier, old snow—from an area very rapidly and redeposit it in "wind shadows," or lees. Moderate winds can do the same but take longer to erode hard snow. Above treeline and in other places where large areas are exposed to the wind, small amounts of snow can make significant wind slab deposits. A rough guideline is that the amount of snow available for transport by strong winds is about equal to the depth to which your feet penetrate while walking.

Cornices form when windblown snow accumulates on the lee sides of ridgetops. Though they can break off and bring tons of snow down on travelers and slopes below, they are often more of a hazard for climbers on the ridge. Cornices can develop into large, overhanging waves of wind slab that hide the true location of the ridge. Climbers may unknowingly step onto the overhanging snow and sometimes plunge through or break off the cornice.

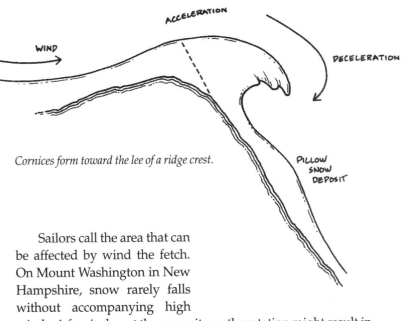

Cornices form toward the lee of a ridge crest.

Sailors call the area that can be affected by wind the fetch. On Mount Washington in New Hampshire, snow rarely falls without accompanying high winds. A few inches at the summit weather station might result in sensitive wind slabs of a foot or more in the leeward bowls. In Mount Washington's case, there are several square miles of fetch before there's any place for the wind to drop its speed and deposit its load of snow. The fetch of a slope could be a huge, flat surface like the alpine garden of Mount Washington or, more commonly, the windward slopes, where high winds push snow uphill and drop it on the other side.

Wind slabs can be sensitive to triggering for days after their creation, but they are most dangerous as they are forming or immediately after they form. Wind slabs are often identifiable by the sound they make as you walk across them. A hard wind slab sounds like you're walking across a sea of Styrofoam coffee cups and allows minimal boot penetration. If it sounds hollow underneath as well, take extra care—you have a heavy wind slab over a lighter layer, which is a recipe for an avalanche.

If you are on new snow, periodically check it by doing hand or shovel shears. The bond to the old snow may be good on one part of the slope but poor on another. Determine the direction of the wind that deposited the snow by observing snow plumes off ridgetops or reading the snow surface. Wind deposits snow far more quickly than most storms. If there are moderate to high winds and loose or new snow, a dangerous avalanche slab will be forming somewhere.

In the late spring and summer, the daily heating of the snow by the sun causes most avalanche activity. Firm snow turns to slush minutes after the sun hits it. How fast that transition occurs depends on how hard it froze the night before and the age of the snow. A rule of thumb among skiers is that when the snow is so soft that your foot sinks in past the boot top, it is time to be somewhere else. Wet slides are likely imminent.

Even when it is cloudy, the snow can heat up to the point where it will slide. Any air temperatures above freezing—in sun or shade—increase snow surface heating and melting. When the air temperature is very warm, wet slides may not be confined to slope aspects that are in the sun.

Rain has a rapid destabilizing effect on new snow. Sustained rain can break down the bonds between the snow grains, causing avalanches that extend deeper into the snowpack. This is particularly true in the spring.

The Human Factor. A recent study by the Colorado Avalanche Information Center indicated that 73 percent of the people killed by avalanches in the United States between 1981 and 1996 had some degree of avalanche training. Another avalanche forecaster states: "We have met the enemy and the enemy is us." There are several factors that can lead mountaineers to put themselves at greater risk than necessary. Often a mountaineer's level of acceptable risk is higher than it should be. Justifying risk taking with rationales such as "climbing is inherently dangerous" causes some people to take chances that a different attitude would lead them to avoid. The signs that the snow stability is poor are subtle, and they are easily ignored when one wants to ski or climb.

Some people develop a false sense of security from being roped up or on belay. Some protection may hold you in place if a small surface sluff knocks you off your feet, but even the best belay is no match for the force of a large avalanche.

Trying to keep on schedule leads some people to take greater risks—the trip is coming to a close, and food, fuel, and time are becoming scarce. But the snow doesn't change for the better just because you want it to.

Another factor is often fatigue. Climbing the extra 600 vertical feet to avoid the 39-degree convex slope leading back to camp may seem daunting at the end of a long climbing day. Don't let tired legs and sore shoulders make you take risks that you wouldn't have considered at the start of the day.

Then there's the "first sunny day syndrome." You've spent four soggy days in a tent, and the skies have finally cleared to 100-mile visibility. Everything is pristine, and you're ready to go. Unfortunately, this is probably a time to wait; the snow needs time to stabilize by either sliding or bonding.

Use the following guidelines to help you evaluate the level of avalanche risk when in the mountains:

- Snow falling at a rate of 1 inch per hour or greater causes instability because the weight is added to the snowpack at a faster rate than the snowpack can easily absorb.
- Snow that falls 1 inch per hour for twelve hours or more causes instability because of the total weight of the new snow.
- Storms that begin cold then become warmer cause instability because heavy snow falls on top of lighter or weaker snow, which may fail to support it.
- Winds of 10 miles per hour or greater during a storm cause instability on leeward slopes.
- Slopes are most unstable during a storm and up to twenty-four hours afterward. Avoid travel at these times. Condi-

tions may remain unsafe for a period of hours or through-out the rest of the season.

If you choose to cross a slope that could slide, consider some of the following precautions to reduce your party's exposure to the hazard:

1. Wear an avalanche transceiver, carry an avalanche probe, and know the appropriate search procedures with both transceivers and probes.
2. Each person should carry a stout shovel for digging victims out of the snow.
3. If you must cross an avalanche slope, select a route that does not cut along lines of weakness in the snowpack and that will minimize your exposure to hazard if an avalanche occurs.
4. Cross the slope quickly and be careful not to fall. Don extra clothing, remove wrists from lanyards, and unfasten waist belts and sternum straps so you will be able to get out of your pack if necessary. If a slide should occur, try to stay on the surface of the snow.
5. Cross slopes one person at a time. Others can visually "spot" and keep track of the last point that person was seen to speed a search in the event of an avalanche.
6. Know the weather history and study the snowpack. Before venturing into the backcountry, call the avalanche forecasters for up-to-date information.

If you or members of your party do get caught in an avalanche, use the following tactics in your attempt to survive:

1. Try to escape the avalanche by stepping or skiing out of its path.
2. Try to get free of packs, ski poles, skis, and any other encumbrance. These will only serve to drag you down into the avalanche.
3. Make every effort to stay afloat in the slide. Try to keep from being dragged deep into the snow, so when the avalanche finally stops, you will not be buried deeply.
4. As the snow begins to stop moving, try to create an air space near your face. Many avalanche victims die from

suffocation. Reach for the snow surface with one arm in hopes of making yourself visible to searchers.

Avalanches are unpredictable. Make travel decisions in avalanche terrain more clear by first identifying all possible avalanche slopes and paths. Evaluate conditions and estimate the level of hazard for slopes or paths you want to cross. Finally, either avoid the slope or path completely or, if you choose to cross one, take appropriate precautions.

SUBJECTIVE HAZARDS

Subjective hazards are hazards that we bring with us into the mountains—the human factor. There is an ongoing relationship between the climber and the natural world. The distant sounds of falling rock may disturb concentration, incessant winds may rattle the nerves, and a near miss can make you weak in the knees. But even without the influence of such factors, human beings still make mistakes of all kinds. Human error, in one form or another, contributes to almost every mountaineering accident. Often the error precedes the accident by a long period of time. Accidents can have complex histories.

It is impossible to separate objective from subjective hazards completely. We play a role in avoiding, preventing, or sometimes even causing many objective hazards. For an understanding of what sorts of accidents are most common, read *Accidents in North American Mountaineering*. The accounts tell of rockfall and avalanche, but most frequently they cite human error. The book's editor, Jed Williamson, lists a number of potentially unsafe acts and errors in judgment that contribute to accidents in the mountains. Unsafe acts are usually a function of a lack of skill or knowledge. They include poor position; improper procedure; inadequate food, water, clothing, or equipment; and unsafe speed. Errors in judgment make up a sneakier category of subjective hazards. The desire to please others, sticking to a schedule, the inability to cope effectively with unexpected situations, misperceptions, fatigue, and distraction are all included in the list of subjective hazards that affect a mountaineer's ability to make sound, timely decisions.

Such errors stem largely from a propensity for choosing actions for the wrong reasons. What, really, are your mountaineering objectives and why? Are you climbing to prove something? Is your objective to be on the plane back home on time or to climb the peak and avoid injury? Take the time to clearly prioritize goals and objectives. Do they include safety, friendship, fun? Before beginning a mountain expedition, spend some time thoroughly discussing goals. Keep them in mind throughout the trip and with every decision made. Do not allow your desire for the climbing objective to color your assessment of the risks and prudent actions.

The most important judgments you will make have to do with both your own and other team members' condition. Your abilities, your knowledge, and whether you are having a bad day can be difficult to judge accurately. Develop a habit of introspection. Discuss subjective variables with expedition members. Allow these subjective factors to influence your judgments. At a minimum, they will help define the true goals of your expedition; at a maximum, they may help you prevent an accident.

3

Climbing Movement

If you already have adequate navigation and camping skills, basic hiking and traveling abilities are enough to take you to some beautiful wild places and spectacular summits. Many mountaineers find this level of difficulty and commitment comfortable and enjoy the mountains throughout their lives without ever using a rope or venturing onto steeper terrain. Don't be coerced into a climbing style or a mountaineering objective more advanced or technical than you are comfortable with. What the British call "hill-walking" and the French, *randonee,* is the most basic and free form of mountaineering. No ropes, few encumbrances, just you, fresh air, and beautiful scenery.

Whether scrambling up moderate peaks or climbing more difficult, technical routes, all mountaineers use the same movement skills. The ability to judge terrain and move or climb over it without falling is the climber's first and most important safety system. Movement skills are the first line of defense against a fall. The rope systems climbers build as they go are secondary systems that conservative climbers would rather not test.

There are certainly situations in which climbers choose climbing problems near the limit of or even beyond their abilities. It is exciting and challenging and fun. The possibility of a fall and the potential inadequacies of any belay make such ambition less appealing in remote locales.

There are three elements that can help you climb safely and within your abilities:

1. An accurate assessment of your abilities.
2. The experience to judge terrain and choose a safe route.

3. The movement skills to climb over that terrain efficiently and without falling.

Experiment in safe situations, and learn the limits of your abilities at practice crags, on boulders near the ground, or with a top rope. These limits change with the level of exposure, weather conditions, and hundreds of other variables. Avoid accidents by accurately judging and estimating abilities, admitting your limits, and staying within them.

FEAR

One of the first problems you must confront in learning to climb is fear. It is a healthy and valuable emotion whose purpose is to keep you alive. Irrational fears can debilitate the novice and make it difficult to get started. My old friend Mike Donahue explains: "There are really two climbs going on, one on the mountain and another in your mind. For the most part, climbing the mountain is the easier of the two. It is the mental climb that is far more difficult. It is as if there is a voice in your head filling it with negative thoughts and saying, 'You can't do this . . . this is too scary. . . . ' " That voice serves a purpose, however. Fear and apprehension help keep you out of danger, and a lack of fear can put a climber at greater risk. So listen to your fears, and ask yourself whether they are real or imagined. Know that you are safe or learn why you are not. If you are not safe, do something about it.

If you cannot be hurt, even if you slip or fall, your fears are irrational. You can learn to control such fears and concentrate on how you move. As a student of mine once put it, "It's not that I want to eliminate the butterflies in my stomach, but that I want to get them to fly in formation."

SAFETY

At NOLS the initial movement classes are usually called bouldering, because we climb around on boulders and rocks. When bouldering, stay low on the rocks. If you become uncomfortable, simply step down onto the ground and relax. Bouldering usually serves as practice in preparation for longer ascents. For some, bouldering is so enjoyable and rewarding that it is all the climbing they care to do. But even when climbing near the ground, there are some safety considerations.

RATINGS OF CLIMBS

Climbers have established a basic vocabulary to help each other be aware of how difficult a climb is before embarking. This communication helps climbers avoid getting into situations that are too difficult and could be dangerous. Routes vary in length and difficulty, and various ratings measure or compare how hard different climbs are.

For rock, the Yosemite decimal system is used in the United States. Different systems are used in other countries. The Yosemite decimal system uses two components: grade and class.

The grade, designated by a Roman numeral from I to VII, indicates the overall length of a climb and the time and number of pitches needed for its ascent. The time is an estimate based on a competent party of two. If your party is larger, or if you know the climb will be quite difficult for you, you may need to allow more time. This is a useful but highly subjective system. Different individuals assign the ratings, and there is quite a bit of latitude within a single grade.

Grade I: one to two hours, involving one to two pitches.

Grade II: two hours to half a day; usually two to five pitches.

Grade III: most of the day; four to ten pitches.

Grade IV: a long day, perhaps starting and descending in the dark; seven to twelve pitches.

Grade V: one night spent on the route; nine to eighteen pitches.

Grade VI: two or more nights spent on the route; fifteen or more pitches.

Grade VII: a new grade that indicates giant, difficult climbs, usually at high altitude.

The class, designated by a number from 1 to 5, indicates the technical difficulty of the climb.

(continued)

RATINGS OF CLIMBS continued

Class 1: walking and easy hiking.

Class 2: difficult hiking, such as through boulder fields, where more balance is required.

Class 3: scrambling, where you must use your hands; may be exposed.

Class 4: exposed, roped climbing with anchors placed every pitch; less experienced climbers are belayed.

Class 5: steep, difficult terrain; roped climbing with fixed belay anchors, where the leader places intermediate pieces of protection.

Class 5 is further divided into a scale of 5.0 to 5.14, 5.0 being the easiest and 5.14 the most gymnastically difficult climb.

Note: Beginning with 5.10, number grades are subdivided into a, b, c, and d before proceeding to the next number grade. There is a huge difference between 5.10a and 5.10d. (Some books use a plus and minus system, instead. A 5.10– is equivalent to 5.10a–b, and a 5.10+ is equivalent to a 5.10c–d.)

Many approaches to mountaineering routes are designated 3rd or 4th Class. There are no hard and fast rules as to when to belay; this decision depends on the climbers' abilities, the weather, and the condition of the route. Some people would definitely feel more comfortable being roped or spotted in exposed 3rd Class terrain, and a leader may choose to place protection in ascending a 4th Class pitch. Just because the guidebook says a climb is 3rd class doesn't mean you should never get out the rope. Ask yourself what the consequences of a fall would be. Note also that 3rd Classing is a term some expert climbers use in describing a solo, ropeless ascent of a 5th Class route.

(continued)

RATINGS OF CLIMBS continued

In addition to Classes 1 through 5, there is a class for artificial aid, designated by an A. A1 is the easiest aid climbing; A2, A3, A4, and A5 progressively become more difficult, more committing, and require more specialized equipment.

Note: There is also a system of C1 through C5 for rating "clean" artificial aid climbs (i.e., without pitons). Both C5 and A5 routes involve 40 to 50 feet of precarious placements that will just barely support body weight; if one placement fails, everything goes, meaning certain injury or death.

A climb's rating is based on the single most difficult move for the lead climber. If a climber is leading a 5.7 climb, most of the climbing may be 5.5 to 5.6 with a single crux move of 5.7. On the other hand, another 5.7 climb may involve many 5.7 moves over the length of the route. There are exceptions to this; for instance, at Devil's Tower in Wyoming, where difficulties are notoriously sustained, a 5.11 climb might contain only 5.10 moves. Overall, however, the pitch gives the feeling of a 5.11.

Some climbs have, in addition to the 5th Class rating, a protection rating, particularly if the climb is poorly protected. An R designates a climb that is "run out" (meaning a gap of 15 feet or more where the leader can't place any protection) and has the potential for a serious fall. If a route in the guidebook is rated 5.9R, it may be best to avoid it. An X rating is even more dangerous; there is a long space of unreliable protection, with the possibility of death in the event of a fall. A few climbing areas also have G and PG ratings, for good and pretty good protection; these notations are quite helpful in selecting a route.

Ice climbs have a different rating system used to describe technical difficulty. Unlike rock, ice is constantly changing and can be steeper, thinner, or more brittle on some days than others. Therefore, ratings used for ice are merely a general guide. *(continued)*

RATINGS OF CLIMBS continued

Water Ice I: low-angle water ice.
Water Ice II: 50- to 70-degree water ice slabs.
Water Ice III: 70-degree moderately angled ice.
Water Ice IV: 80-degree water ice; steep, may contain short vertical steps.
Water Ice V: 90-degree water ice; long vertical sections. Usually, protection is good.
Water Ice VI: vertical ice in combination with thin ice or free-hanging icicles. Poor or marginal protection.

Note: The VII rating, first used in the Canadian Rockies, designates thin vertical ice of doubtful adhesion to the rock.

Also, there is now a rating system for mixed ice and rock that grades routes from M1 through M8/9. (An M7 feels like a 5.11–12, an M8 like a 5.12–13. These routes always involve the technique of dry tooling.)

When choosing a climb, use the rating to get an idea of how hard the route is, then study it and decide for yourself. When climbing at a new area, it's a good idea to do some climbs well within your ability to get a feel for the rating scale and the style of climbing.

Ratings are a helpful means of communication, but it is important to remember what they do not communicate: They do not describe danger or exposure, nor do they give any information about the beauty or quality of a route. You must, in the end, rely on your own ability to accurately assess a climb.

Choose a safe site, preferably free of rockfall and other hazards. Choose solid rock so pieces won't break off when you pull or stand on holds. It is best if the landing is flat to prevent the risk of turning your ankle when you step back down to it. If you plan to climb up onto the top of a boulder, scout it first to make sure you'll be able to get off. On ice and snow, practice movement at sites with safe runouts where you can slide to a stop.

Don't wear jewelry. Rings, necklaces, and watches can get hung up on holds and cause injury.

Boulder with a spotter—a partner who stands below you as you move on the rock. A spotter is always ready and can guide you gently to the ground if you come off the rock unexpectedly. Spotters should not try to catch climbers. Rather, their job is to guide them to a safe landing, with special attention to protecting the head. Spotters can also offer contact from below to help you stay on the rock or slide down to the ground under control. They are valuable for moral support and occasional coaching if you ask for it.

MOVEMENT ON ROCK

Climbing is a skill you either presently possess or lost through lack of practice while growing up. We are all born with some basic climbing ability, but as we grow older, fears develop and skills deteriorate. Rock is an excellent place to start relearning movement skills, because the medium is predictable.

Endurance will be crucial when you move onto longer climbs. Fear can be one of the most insidious drains on energy, but poor technique can also deplete your reserves. The best climbers have made a science of energy conservation and use their bodies with extraordinary efficiency. This requires that they know their bodies well and react immediately to the messages they send. The basic tenets are simple: Regular breathing keeps muscles perfused with oxygen; big muscles, such as those in the legs and back, can do more work than smaller ones; and the skeleton does not tire.

Rock climbing consists, very generally, of two skill areas: face climbing and crack climbing. Face climbing across blank sections is a natural sort of climbing that is relatively easy to learn. You find the biggest edges and holds and choose the best way to push, pull, and balance on them. Crack climbing requires more learning. Crack master Dale Bard calls it "the most unnatural form of free climbing" in which "most of the techniques are not obvious and are based on camming, counter pressure, or subtle leverage."

In reality, climbing usually involves a bit of both techniques. Footwork is the most subtle and important aspect of either and is most easily learned on low-angle face climbs, so start there.

FACE-CLIMBING TECHNIQUES

Face-climbing techniques are not advanced, and novices often have great success on low-angle, seemingly blank faces with only a small amount of instruction.

Strength, Flexibility, and Balance

Keep most of your body weight on your feet, and concentrate on the smooth transfer of your weight from foot to foot. Consider the various movement options, and choose moves that maintain balance over one or both feet. Seek positions in which you can relax most of your muscles. Feel the tension in your shoulders, and take the time to drop them and relax them.

Small steps allow for easier, more balanced weight transfers. When terrain calls for longer steps, climbers counterbalance with another body part to push in the opposite direction of the step or reach. Flexibility increases options and allows even more freedom to be creative. As terrain steepens and becomes more difficult, strength plays a more important role.

Footwork

You will develop footwork skills far more quickly by using a pair of modern rock shoes with sticky rubber soles. If you plan on using them in the backcountry, get a pair that fits snugly with a light pair of socks. Consult a local mountain shop, and buy a pair that will be useful in both crack and face climbing.

Watch skilled climbers on the rock. Note how much of their time is spent looking down at their feet and how quiet those feet become once placed on the holds.

Gain purchase on small ledges and flakes by edging: Look closely at the hold you choose and, with your eyes, center it under the ball of your foot and fit as much of the edge of your boot on the hold as possible. Stand up. If the hold is less distinct, more like a small section of lower-angled rock, smear as much of the rubber on the bottom of your boot onto it as possible. Again, stand up. If you are faced with a crack, place your boot narrowly into the crack, then twist to widen the profile into a secure posi-

tion; this is known as jamming. Start by playing around with edging and smearing; save foot and toe jams for later. Realize that most of the time you are not just edging or smearing but doing a bit of both.

The inside edge, under the big toe, is your strongest and generally most effective edge. It is here that most climbing shoes wear out first. The outside edge can be used to help you pull closer to the rock and reach higher.

Be slow and methodical with your first steps on rock. From the beginning, you create habits that will stay with you for a long time; be sure they are good ones. Look for and choose each foothold, and place the boot on it precisely. Look at your feet when you move them. Place a foot in its best position, feel the foothold through the

With hands low, a climber can position his body over his feet. This pushes his body weight directly onto his feet, adding friction to smears and edges.

shoe, and then don't move it. Analyze each placement, considering why it works and how it might work even better.

As you analyze your foot placements, you will find that their security is based largely on how much weight you can put over them. Edging is based on balancing your weight directly over that little edge. Lean too far in (you will feel weight coming onto your hands) and the foot slips off. Smearing is based on friction. The more weight you put directly over that boot, pushing down into it, the more friction there will be between the boot and the rock. Friction must be actively applied through your feet and onto the rock; don't be tentative. Pushing harder on your feet usually helps.

Hands

Manage your body position over your feet with your hands. Handholds can be almost anything: a big jug, a small edge, a tiny crystal, a pocket, or a hole in the rock of almost any size.

Standing on good holds near the ground, relax and get comfortable. Rest. Now experiment. Reach a bit higher to grab a handhold. Now another, even higher. Do you feel more of your body's weight coming onto your arms? As your arms take more weight, your legs take less. If you reach too high, your feet will slip off their holds.

Generally, on anything but vertical or overhanging rock, hands are used only as balance points. Use your palms below your waist to take the weight off a foot while you move it. This is known as palming, and it allows you to lean one way or the other in order to put your foot where you want it.

When pulling on tiny edges, you can use a few tricks to add to the strength of your hands. First, fit as many fingers as possible onto the edge or crystal. Fingers work well together, and four fingers are stronger than the simple sum of their parts. Involve the thumb whenever possible. Lay it over other fingers or press it up to the side of the index finger. Try not to overgrip. Pull only as much as is necessary to keep your body where you want it and still conserve energy. Try not to pull by bending your elbow. Pull your shoulder back instead, and allow the strength of your torso to do the work.

Whenever one hand is on a large hold and the other can be taken off the rock, let it hang down below your heart to relax for a moment. If you leave your hands in one flexed position for long, they will tire; if left for too long, they will not recover quickly. Rest them for short periods as frequently as possible so they don't get so pumped that they cannot regain their strength.

CRACK-CLIMBING TECHNIQUES

Climbing cracks in the rock is a bit more advanced than low-angle face climbing. Proficiency with these techniques is important because most of the time you will follow crack systems up the rocky peaks. In the wilderness, we place our protection in cracks and rarely stray far from their security.

Upward movement comes from the feet and legs. Use your eyes to find the holds rather than blindly searching by feel. Whenever possible, rest on your skeleton. What is different in crack technique is how the climber grasps the rock.

Gain purchase in cracks with variations of a technique called jamming. Foot jams, hand jams, finger jams, fist jams—even knees and whole arms get jammed in cracks. In theory, the techniques are simple: Put a body part in the crack in its narrowest orientation, and then twist or flex it into a wider orientation to fill the crack. It helps if the crack narrows a bit below the jam.

Jamming may sound painful, and I must admit that it can be. It may also feel very insecure to begin with. Eventually you will find hand and foot jams to be some of the most secure and comfortable holds available, but this takes time and practice. Don't injure or discourage yourself by trying problems that are too difficult. Start on easier terrain, and train yourself to be methodical, fluid, and successful. Don't start on difficult problems, or you will train yourself to be sloppy and jerky. You will also cut your hands as you slip around on jams.

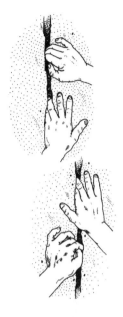

Tips jam: *A difficult jam when nothing larger can be found. The right hand is thumb down; lowering the elbow expands and cams the fingers more securely against the rock. This creates a camming effect, making the jam more secure. The left hand is inserted thumb up in a "pinkie jam"; this will work in the smallest cracks. Wedge the fingers and then cam them by raising the elbow.*

Fingerlock: *A secure jam using the entire finger up to the knuckle. The right hand is placed thumb down, and the fingers are stacked on top of the index. Again, the hand is cammed by lowering the elbow. The left hand demonstrates a jam for slightly wider cracks, incorporating the thumb in a "thumb cam" and stacking the fingers on top of it. Feet are often on face holds when climbing thin cracks. Also look for flares in which the toe can fit.*

Hand jam: *The most secure and comfortable jam. The hand shown is inserted thumb up, with straight fingers. The fingers and the meaty part of the palm are pushed against one side of the crack, and the back of the hand against the other side. This way, the hand can expand to fit the size of the crack. A thumb-down jam will fit in a slightly smaller crack, and lowering the elbow will cam it into place. It will start feeling less secure as the body moves up and the elbow swings out. In corner cracks you will find it most effective for one hand to be thumb up and the other thumb down.*

Fist jam: *This jam is for cracks too wide for hand jams—it tends to feel ratty but it does work! Make a fist and insert it in the crack, preferably above a constriction, then flex the hand muscles to expand it. For a larger crack the thumb can be positioned to the side of the fist, tip against the index finger.*

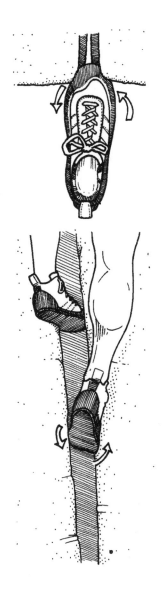

Toe jam: *A very secure foot jam used in conjunction with hand jams. Insert the toe of the boot in the crack with the big toe up and knee off to the side, then roll the knee up and straighten the leg. This jam is difficult to remove if the foot has been inserted too deeply in the crack; try to keep the ball of the foot out of most cracks. For slightly wider cracks the foot can be slotted straight in. The toes can also be inserted big toe down, with the foot angled sideways to utilize the little toe and outside of the foot. With cracks where both feet and hands are in the same crack, take care not to place feet too high. By keeping your feet low, your body will stay closer to the rock with weight over your feet.*

Offwidth: *For cracks too wide for jams with the hand, yet too small to insert one's body. Ascending offwidths can be slow and laborious. It is helpful to wear long-sleeved shirts and heavy pants. The climber on the left is using an arm lock with the inside arm. The shoulder and upper arm are pushing on one side of the crack, and the palm is pushing on the oppo-site side. The outside arm*

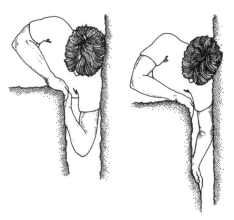

is pulling out on the edge of the crack, and the climber's back is against the off-set side of the crack. The climber on the right is using the same techniques in combination with an arm bar. Again, the shoulder, upper arm, and elbow are pushing against one side of the crack and the palm against the other side. Push-ing down from the shoulder with this arm creates more leverage.

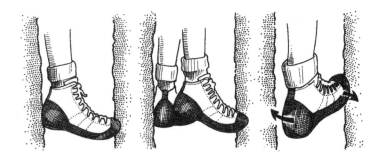

Foot jams for offwidth cracks. *The right sketch illustrates the toe and heel torqued against the sides of the crack (either side of the foot will work) to create friction. As the crack widens, a full toe-heel jam can slot in (left). Knees can also be jammed (be careful of getting them stuck), and the whole leg can be used similarly to an arm bar. If the crack is offset, the outside leg can take advantage of any stems or holds on the outside face. It can also be bent in a chimneying position, with the foot pushing against the same wall as the climber's back. Once the crack is too wide for toe-heel jams, foot stacks must be used (center).*

The climber on the left is in a flaring offwidth. By staying on the outside and resisting the urge to get sucked into the back of the crack, he is more flexible and mobile, has more weight on his feet, and can use some chimney technique with the outside leg to aid in upward motion. Note the torqued toe-heel position and the arm bar with the inside extremities. The climber on the right is in a chimney; now the crack is wide enough for the entire body. The back is against the steeper side of the chimney, while both hands and feet are in opposition on the other side, in a rest position. To move, the right foot should be brought up as high as possible, while the left foot is placed below the buttocks, as shown. By pushing and wriggling, the climber can gain elevation. Next, the feet are switched, and the process is repeated. Arms can be on either wall, wherever they feel most useful. There are different chimney sizes—a squeeze chimney is a narrow chimney in which the climber must use the knees; in a classic chimney, knees need not be used and bruised, because the feet can do all the work. The climber in the sketch has taken advantage of a flaring chimney by finding an arm lock on the inside.

COMBINING TECHNIQUES

Counterpressure means simply to push or pull in opposite directions. It allows the climber to put weight or energy onto feet or hands and use holds that face sideways. A classic application of counterpressure is liebacking. By pulling on one side of a crack, the climber can put a great deal more weight onto the feet, allowing them to stick to less featured, vertical walls. Liebacking requires the hands to oppose the feet, so the technique can tire the arms quickly. With experimentation, you will find you can build various forms of counterpressure into much of your climbing. If it is used gently with other techniques, it is not nearly so tiring.

When liebacking, climbers pull with their hands and push with their feet. The added weight on their feet allows them to use steeper footholds.

Stemming is a useful counterpressure technique that involves pushing outward with both feet at the same time. When stemming, the climber is balancing over both feet, and it is impossible to pick one of them up. In order to move a foot, counterpressure must be provided with a hand. Wide inside corners and large chimneys are perfect for pure stemming. It can also be used in many other situations. You will find, for example, that you can stem between two small face holds with hands or feet. It is one of the most common tactics for resting on steep rock and is a practical way to conserve energy.

One day at our local crag, a climber was having a difficult time with a particular move. He could not reach the large handhold he wanted, no matter what he tried. His partner suggested that he dangle one foot off in the opposite direction from the handhold, a technique known as flagging, and then try again.

Use stemming—counterpressure between the feet—to get your body weight over your feet in steep dihedrals. Experiment with stemming on face holds.

Flagging is an extreme example of counterbalance in which a reach in one direction is countered by the weight of a leg in the other, allowing the balance of the climber's weight to remain over a foothold.

Without much faith, the climber reluctantly took the suggestion and found that he could easily lean out and grab the jug. By counterbalancing with the weight of a leg in one direction, he was able to lean much farther in the other.

You will find counterbalancing useful with almost every move. It can be extreme, as in the example above, or very subtle. Frequently climbers choose smaller holds to facilitate counterbalance and allow a reach that might otherwise be impossible.

REST

Climbing demands the use of muscles and body positions that we are not accustomed to in everyday life. As a result, the search for resting spots is very important. Climbers move from resting spot to resting spot.

Use your bones. Try to rest on your skeleton rather than on tensed muscles. Stand tall on straight legs, hang down on straight arms. I once watched another climber, Lynn Hill, succeed on a route that I had struggled with. My arms always failed near the top. She hardly ever bent her arms on an overhanging climb. She twisted her body and used her shoulders, hips, and abdominal muscles to raise her hand to the next hold.

Whenever you get into a new position on the rock, try to fine-tune it into the most restful and relaxed pose possible. This usually entails figuring out how to rest on the skeleton while relaxing the muscles. Lower your heels or put one on a large hold to relax the calves. Straighten the elbow to relax the biceps. Hook a heel on an overhang to take weight from the hands.

When you must rely on muscles instead of bones, try to use them in their most powerful orientations. Many muscles, the biceps for example, are more effective when fully contracted than they are in intermediate positions. Therefore, when pulling up with your arms, try to move quickly from hanging from a straight arm to full contraction or a "lock-off," and then back to a straight arm as soon as possible. The upward motion should come from the feet.

Your small muscles are the most challenging to rest. The muscles in your forearms are involved in almost every move. Taken to the limits of their usefulness, they fail and take many minutes to recover. Avoid letting forearms get to this stage by resting fingers frequently. The rest does not have to be long to be effective; sometimes just a little shake below the heart will do. But the rest must come when it is needed.

MOVEMENT ON SNOW

When climbing on snow, footwork is again the foundation. Use mountaineering boots for snow climbing. Stiff-soled, leather hiking boots work well and are more comfortable during approach hikes; plastic-shelled mountaineering boots are generally warmer and better for cold weather climbing. Instead of the hands on snow, climbers employ a tool so essential to mountaineering that it seems to be the sport's symbol: the ice ax.

For general mountaineering on snow and low-angle ice, a standard 60- to 70-centimeter-long ice ax is best. Used incorrectly, these tools are dangerous, so take the time to learn the right way to use them. A standard ax has a spike at the end of the main shaft, which is held on by a ferrule. The spike is meant to be plunged deeply into soft snow or used as a balance point on harder surfaces. At the other end is the head of the ax, which consists of a pick for purchase on steep ice and an adze for chopping. There is also a carabiner hole to which you may attach a leash.

Parts of the Ice Ax

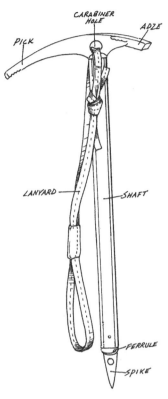

When simply carrying the ax but not using it, carry it horizontally by the shaft, with the pick pointing down and behind you and the spike out in front. When climbing low- to moderate-angle snow, carry the ax by its head, in self-arrest position—one hand over the head of the ax with the pick to the rear. The thumb lies under the adze.

The ice ax is used as a climbing tool to aid progress and improve balance. Plunged into the snow, it also serves as an anchor that can be replaced with each step. On low-angle slopes, an ax that is too short forces climbers to lean into the mountain to plunge the spike into the snow. In the same way that leaning into a rock face causes your feet to slip, leaning into a snow slope will make your boots slide out from under you. On steeper slopes, climbers prefer shorter axs because they are easier to manipulate in more complex techniques. An ax that is too long is hard to lift out of the snow and is heavy and unwieldy on steep snow and ice.

There is no consensus among mountaineers about whether or not to leash the ice ax to the harness or wrist during travel. Certainly, there are situations in which the climber would not want to be attached to the ax, as it might stab or cut during a bad fall. The famous British expeditioner Chris Bonnington tells how not having his ax attached prevented fatal wounds from the pick, adze, and spike during a fall. When I fell off Mount Foraker in 1984, my ax was leashed to my wrist, and I was stabbed several times. I did not lose my ax, but I have never used a leash since.

In some situations, however, such as during glacier travel, on mixed climbs, or when cutting steps, a leash offers the climber a great advantage. Travel in glaciated terrain demands an ice ax, and one cannot afford to lose it in a crevasse fall. A long leash, from the ax to the climber's harness, prevents it from being lost and facilitates its use as a handy self-belay anchor. On mixed ground, the climber may want to let go of the ax at times in order to make use of handholds. A leash, or lanyard, to the wrist is very helpful here.

I find lanyards tedious on snow because of the frequency with which I change hands on the ax. Of course, without a lanyard, dropping the ax is not an option. Whether or not you are wearing a lanyard, make holding on to the ax second nature. Always keep a firm hold on the ax, no matter what the situation or hand position.

SNOW CLIMBING

Principles for climbing on snow are similar to those that apply to movement on rock—climb with the feet, and use the ax for balance. When climbing snow, your boots are always edging. The difference is that you can put the edges anywhere you want. Your hands don't usually touch the snow. Instead, a well-placed spike makes your ax serve as a cane, adding a balance point when you step.

In most snow-climbing situations, you have the advantage of being able to stop yourself if you slip. Self-arrest techniques can stop a slip or fall on snow but have limitations. For every individual, there will be a limit to the steepness and condition of the terrain on which arrest is possible. On K2, one of my partners fell off, and his inability to self-arrest likely caused his death. Learn the limits of your abilities before facing the decision of whether or not you can arrest on a given slope. Practice the techniques illustrated here so you'll be able to stop yourself when you are sliding down a snow slope in any position. As with riding a bike, muscles learn these skills more so than brains. Train your body by repeated practice to react immediately with the correct technique. Revisit these fundamentals frequently, no matter how superior you believe your abilities to be.

Self-arrest position consists of pointing the toes of your boots and the pick of your ax into the snow. Feet should be about shoulder width, bottom high in the air, forcing your upper body weight onto the head of your ax. Hold the ax in self-arrest position securely, and pull the spike high out of the snow with the other hand near the ferrule. If you are sliding on your belly, just pop up into this position.

If you are sliding on your back, roll toward the head of the ax. This ensures that the pick will hit the snow first and begin slowing you down and improving your position immediately.

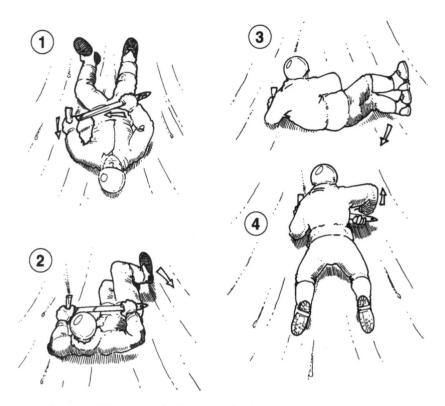

If you are sliding on your back with your head down, plant the pick near your hip and allow your hips and legs to rotate away. Pull yourself into position as you slow.

In the unlikely event that you are falling face first, place the pick far out to one side (even farther than shown) and kick your legs around downhill, then pull yourself into position.

Soloing across easier snow slopes, there are three lines of defense against a long fall: your climbing ability, your use of a self-belay by plunging the shaft into the snow, and your ability to self-arrest if you do fall.

Practice snow skills on a moderately angled snow slope that runs out to a flat snow surface below. Here, if you fall and cannot stop yourself, you will slide out to the flats and slow to a stop.

Several basic foot techniques are all you need to climb on any snow slope. The first is simple walking. With feet flat against the snow surface, the ice ax is held like a cane, with one hand in self-arrest position. As the slope steepens, you will begin to carve out steps by kicking and standing on the edge of the boot.

Splay your feet out and gain purchase on the snow with the inside edges of the boots to duckfoot straight up moderate slopes. Hold the head of the ax in self-arrest position, and use it like a cane in front of you. If the terrain is tricky and you feel insecure, plunge the shaft into the snow with each step. If you slip, a well-placed ax might serve as a handhold that you can grab (low on the shaft) to prevent a fall. This is a form of self-belay that is very effective on snow. If the terrain is steeper, place both hands on the ax's head and plunge it more deeply to add security.

Another form of edging, called traversing, is executed by keeping the ice ax in the uphill hand. Place it securely enough that it can be planted quickly if your feet slip, but do not lean on the ax, which will cause your feet to slide out from under you. Each step should gain the same amount of elevation. In order to accomplish this, the downhill foot must cross up and over the uphill foot to kick a step. When you look back at the steps, they should each look the same, as if each could have been made with either foot.

A more balanced method, the box step, provides for gaining elevation with the uphill foot and then placing the downhill foot at the same elevation. This is easier for the leader but demands that all who follow must be in sync.

To make steps, carve out an edge with the toe of the boot, and then slide the heel of the boot into place as the kick ends. The edge you create should be perfectly perpendicular to the fall line of the slope. Usually a step is made with the first kick, although

As a snow slope steepens, the climber employs a progression of techniques from walking (not shown), to duckfooting, to traversing, to a combination of duckfooting and front-pointing, and finally to front-pointing with both feet. The ice ax is always in the uphill hand and, on soft snow, kept in self-arrest position. Climbers always vary techniques to use different muscles and avoid overtiring.

On snow, use the edges of your boots. Keep the soles perpendicular to the fall line of the slope. When you look back at the marks made by good steps, a line drawn through the toes of each step will be parallel to a line drawn through the heel of each step.

sometimes two are necessary. Too many kicks wastes energy and time, and you only need a bit of an edge. When you kick the final time, keep the boot still for an instant before standing up on the step. This allows the snow to refreeze. When teams are climbing, each person uses and improves upon the steps made by the leader. Those in the rear conserve energy by not having to make their own steps. When the leader tires, others can take over kicking steps.

When traversing, there are positions of balance or rest and positions that are out of balance. When the uphill foot is in the high step, your body is most in balance, and this is when you should move your ax. Don't move the ax when the downhill foot is crossed over the other and in the high step, because your balance is most tenuous in this position. While traversing, move the ax with every other step, always from the position of balance.

If you find that it takes several kicks to make each step, either the steps are bigger than they need to be, or the snow is too hard and you would do well to put on your crampons and move more quickly. If the section of hard snow is short, chop a few steps in the snow with the ax.

The placement of your steps determines how quickly you gain elevation. If the slope is quite steep and traversing is difficult or insecure, use front-pointing, a technique in which you kick the toes of your boots into the snow. It is an easy technique to learn and allows speedy progress up the slope. It can be more tiring, however, especially for the calves.

An easy way to conserve energy on steep snow is to duck-foot with one boot and front-point with the other. By alternating feet, you won't tire as quickly as when using pure front-pointing. Most of the time, mountaineers mix techniques as the terrain changes or as specific muscles tire.

DESCENDING SNOW

The most secure method for descending snow is the reverse of front pointing. Mountaineers often refer to it as facing in. Much of the time, however, conditions and slope angle allow for speedier descent techniques. The most common and controlled of the techniques that face out is the plunge step.

When using the plunge step, keep body weight out forward over your feet, with toes up so the heels dig into the snow. "Nose over the toes" is the correct body position to prevent a slip, but keep your ice ax in self-arrest position in case you do slip. Bend at the waist and take large steps down the slope, plunging the heel of your boot deeply into the snow. If you want a bit more security, plunge the shaft of your ax in

Plunge step. Keep your weight out over your feet: "Nose over your toes!"

deeply with each step. If you slip, you can hold on to the well-planted ax. This technique works best if you really commit to it. It is difficult to plunge step effectively when tentative.

The fastest—and sometimes least controlled—descent techniques are glissades. If you are a skier, you'll probably take to them quite readily, but if not, they will require some practice. There are three glissade methods: standing, squatting, and sitting. In each of them, keep the ax head in self-arrest position in case you lose control.

A standing glissader skis on his boots. Sitting and squatting glissades allow you to drag the shaft of the ax in the snow as a rudder and brake yet remain ready to roll toward the head of the ax and into a self-arrest.

Glissading can significantly increase a climber's speed in the mountains. A slope that takes an hour to descend by facing in and front-pointing can often be descended in ten minutes by glissading. But beware of letting the prospect of a quick descent lure you into a glissade that is too steep or one with hazards at the bottom, such as cliffs, crevasses, or open water.

MOVEMENT ON ICE

When climbing on snow, mountaineers put ice axes rather than their hands in contact with the medium. On ice the climber is yet further removed from the medium, with axes for hands and crampons for feet.

CRAMPONS

There was a time in mountaineering history, before crampons came on the scene, when climbers had to cut and shape small edges in the ice and then stand up on them in their tricouni nailed boots. This was extraordinarily tedious and demanded impeccable technique. Ice is an unforgiving medium.

Now we use crampons. Most modern crampons have ten points of steel sticking straight down from the bottom and one or two protruding from the front. They are either rigid and meant to be used with rigid boots (plastic mountaineering boots, for example) or hinged for use on lighter, more flexible boots. On very steep ice, climbers prefer a rigid boot and crampon system because there is less vibration and the front points can penetrate deeper into the ice without breaking it away. On lower-angle ice, flexible crampons are adequate. Avoid using rigid crampons on flexible boots, because the crampon may bend and break.

Some crampons have step-in bindings, which are simple and quick but cannot be worn easily with overboots. Donning crampons fitted with straps may be slower, but they are very secure and can be worn with overboots. Whichever type you choose, learn to put the

Lash straps allow you to use one pair of crampons on many different boots. Thread the instep strap from the inside out on the toe eyes. This locks the tension in place and keeps the strap from falling completely forward on the boot.

crampons on securely in two or three minutes, and always carry them in a convenient place. Keep the points sharp.

CLIMBING ICE

Yvon Chouinard wrote an entire book titled *Climbing Ice*. It is worth reading if you are interested in the intricacies of ice climbing, and especially if your goals include climbing frozen waterfalls.

Climbing, descending, and even traversing on low- to moderate-angle ice require a technique logically called flatfooting. This technique involves stomping all ten of the bottom points of the crampons securely into the ice and rotating ankles and knees to keep your weight directly over your feet. Be precise and aggressive; plant the points well. Hold your ice ax in self-arrest position in the uphill hand. On low-angle ice, you will be able to face up the slope and splay your feet out, but don't edge—flatfoot.

As ice steepens, ankles and knees generally cannot maintain all ten points on the ice while facing up the hill. On steeper terrain, you will find that the only way to flatfoot is to point the toes of your boots almost straight down the ice. To make upward progress, you essentially back up the slope. Once turned sideways to the ice or with your back toward it, you will need a different ice ax position, which the French call *piolet ramasse*. From self-arrest position, with the ax in your downhill hand, turn the ax around so that the pick points forward. Then place your other hand low on the shaft. You can hold the ax horizontally at waist height or below and stab the spike into the ice for a point of balance on tough flatfooting moves.

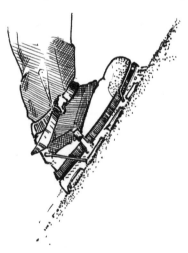

On low-angle ice and for rests on steeper ice, flatfoot. Avoid edging in crampons. Stab as many bottom points into the ice as possible.

You will find, especially after a fair bit of practice, that flat-footing is a fine technique on moderate slopes and for short distances, but on steeper or longer slopes, it just doesn't cut it. Here it is faster and easier to swing your boots and stab the front points straight into the ice. Keep the bottoms of your feet perpendicular to the face. If the heels are too low, they will lever the front points out of the ice; if they are too high, the toes of the boots will prevent full penetration. The swing need not be powerful. Most of the time, the weight of the boot alone will be enough to penetrate the ice, and you will not really need to kick at all.

There is no reason not to use a different technique for each foot. Probably the most common combination is to front-point with one foot and flatfoot with the other. Known as *pied troisième,* this technique is far less tiring than pure front-pointing and is used even on the steepest ice.

When facing the ice and either front-pointing or using the technique *pied troisième,* the climber often places the pick of the ice ax instead of the spike. There are three ways to place the pick. One is to hold the ax with your hand on top of the head and the pick pointing forward. This reverse of self-arrest position allows you to use the pick as a dagger and to place the pick while keeping the hand or hands low and in balance. The pick should be planted deeply enough to add security but not driven in so far that it is difficult to remove. You can also place your wrist and thumb under the adze and wrap your fingers over the head of the ax. This allows you to plant the pick like a dagger at about shoulder height. Be creative with these techniques. For example, place the ax in high-dagger position and then, as you move up, move your hand to the top of the head (low-dagger position).

On the steepest terrain, hold the ax by the shaft, near the ferrule, and swing the pick into the ice. Called *piolet traction,* this is a very secure technique, especially with your wrist in a leash. The leash allows you to rest on your bone structure and grip the ax less tightly, thus saving forearm strength. In *piolet traction,* the pick may be difficult to remove. Wiggle the ax up and down, never sideways; twisting action on the pick may break it, and an

This ice climber is front-pointing with one crampon and flatfooting with the other. The terrain is of an angle that allows him to keep most of the weight on his feet. During the swing the climber's body, especially the feet, should be still and quiet while the arm and shoulder follow through.

ice ax is one of the few items of equipment that are truly impossible to repair in the backcountry.

On very steep ice, you may find that you want the security of a second tool—one for each hand.

Leashes are very useful on ice. A dropped ax will not stick as it might in snow. Realize too that a climber's defenses are significantly reduced on ice as opposed to snow. Many of the ax placements will not be secure enough to provide a true self-belay, and falls are difficult to arrest. In fact, self-arrest on ice is generally not an option.

STEEP ICE

by Rob Hess

As ice becomes more vertical, a climber is more dependent on front-point techniques and an ice ax technique called *piolet traction*. You might consider the definition of "steep ice" as ice on which you feel the need to begin utilizing two ice tools. The steepness and consistency combined with the overall committing nature determine the climb's difficulty.

Softer "alpine ice" is considered easier to place tools in than the more brittle "water ice." The difference between the two is the amount of air held in the frozen water. Ice that is porous with air bubbles is generally softer and whiter in color. Hard ice, with less air in it, is more blue in color. At times it may appear clear like glass.

When an ice slope is between 50 degrees and 90 degrees, a mountaineer becomes more dependent on his ice tools. It is possible to ascend steep ice with only one tool, but keep in mind that it is usually faster, safer, and more secure to climb with a second tool.

Rock climbing and ice climbing are similar in that they utilize the same safety systems; they differ in that you rely on the hands and feet for purchase on rock, whereas on ice you are heavily dependent on your tools. Because ice climbing is so tool-dependent, it is necessary to consider your equipment needs carefully.

Boots are where it all begins. Well-fitted, rigid-soled mountaineering boots give you minimal heel lift and provide the performance needed for steep ice. Ice tool preferences vary greatly. Climbers most commonly use two tools 50 to 60 centimeters long, shorter than a general mountaineering ice ax. As with so many aspects of climbing, the type of tools tends to be a matter of personal preference. I have had the best luck on steep ice with recurve or straight droop picks. I use one

(continued)

STEEP ICE continued

tool with an adze and one with a hammer. In the case of extreme ice climbing, such as vertical waterfall ice, I carry a third tool to use while placing protection and as a backup in the event that one of my primary tools breaks. I fit each tool with a lanyard so that I can hang them from my wrists instead of having to grip the shafts. Basically, this reduces arm pump. Some folks like leashing one of their tools to their harness for extra security, but this can hinder smooth tool placement if the leash is too short.

Crampons are the most vital link in the system and require special care on a continual basis. Learn proper crampon adjustment, and keep the points sharp. I prefer rigid crampons over adjustable ones. Rigid crampons tend not to shatter the ice as much, and they provide more secure placements. Be sure to keep crampon points sharp. A helmet is especially important, as falling ice and debris are common. Bring enough ice screws (eight to ten) to protect a pitch and build two belay anchors. In a wilderness mountaineering setting, consider selecting gear that meets all of your ice-climbing needs.

Choosing a route and the line of ascent is tricky; pick out the weaknesses or easiest paths up the route—lowest angles, places that will allow you to stem with your feet—and look for the most secure ice. Above all, seek options for rest. If leading, I try to climb out and away from the belayer so I will avoid bombing him with ice and other projectiles. I always keep this in mind when setting belays. *Think ahead!*

The fundamentals of steep-ice technique are based on the feet and crampons. As with rock climbing, good footwork is the key to success in ice climbing. Front-pointing tends to be the most strenuous cramponing technique and requires the most concentration; be absolutely sure the frontpoints are well placed. Conservation of energy is vital, so

(continued)

STEEP ICE continued

place crampons with authority, but learn to recognize how hard to swing the foot for the given ice conditions. Think about keeping your heels low when placing a crampon. Seek options for placing the foot and crampon flatfooted to give your calf muscles a break. Stemming from one ice feature to another is also a great way of saving energy with your feet. Try to arrange it so that when you want to place an ice screw for protection, you can take advantage of a terrain feature that provides such options.

Skillful ice tool placement requires a knowledge of the various ice consistencies and the amount of force required to place solid tools in those conditions. Too delicate a placement and the tool will pull out, too hard and you will shatter the surrounding ice. My worst nightmare is pulling up on tools and having them pop off.

As I swing my tool, I look for spots that are more conducive to easy placement. There is nothing like getting a nice, secure *thwack* on your first swing. The best placements are in slight depressions, air bubbles, porous ice, and the tops of small pillars. Don't overlook old tool holes. Any concavity in the ice is likely a good place to aim your pick. After I choose my spot, I visualize an X and concentrate my swing on that spot. Good placement may take numerous pokes, but learn to distinguish what a good placement looks and sounds like: solid!

Realize, however, that placement is only half the battle. Removal of an ice tool for replacement can be as strenuous as placement, if not more so. I often soften or dull the teeth on the bottom side of the pick to assist in removal. This works nicely and does not compromise tool placement security. Be sure that when you do remove the tool, you are careful to loosen the pick with up-and-down movement; torquing side to side will risk breaking your pick.

(continued)

STEEP ICE continued

Once I begin climbing, my attention focuses on the progression and fluidity of my motion. I try to conserve energy whenever possible. Most people have one arm that is stronger and more coordinated than the other. I hold my most effective tool in my weaker hand, because the better tool will lessen the pump in that arm. My less coordinated arm will always stay attached to the tool, while I often take the better-coordinated arm out of my lanyard for protection placement. With two tools securely placed, I work my crampons up as high as possible while keeping my arms straight.

The next step is to stand up and extend my legs, but before doing so I like to loosen the tool that I plan to move first in order to waste less time and energy. Standing tall with my arms bent and my hands at chest level, I am now ready to replace one of my tools higher while the other maintains my hold on the ice. The tool I replace first is a matter of preference, but I like swinging my strong hand first. This makes me feel more confident when I commit to the tool and remove the other. On very sustained steep sections, I shift my hips laterally, thereby shifting weight from one hand to another and allowing the unweighted hand to rest. In a pinch you can hang off your harness on placed tools via some sort of leash to regain strength, but you had better be able to trust your placements.

Though you'll want to get the most height out of each swing, overextending should be avoided, as it tends to pull your crampons out of their stable horizontal position. Be cautious when moving from steep terrain back onto easier. Your arms and body are bent over on moderate terrain, but your feet are still on the steeper. Don't move your tools so high that you can't see your feet. Always maintain a stable platform for your feet, and be creative.

All the objective hazards addressed in this book apply to ice climbs, but the difficulty of an ice climb is the severity of
(continued)

> **STEEP ICE continued**
>
> the lead. The common climbing adage "the leader must not fall" holds true for steep ice; ice is a much less predictable medium than rock, and there is great potential for injury from ice tools and crampons during a fall. While first learning ice climbing, seek climbing options that are top-roped or boulder near the ground. This will give you experience and practice on a variety of consistencies of ice before considering a lead. Safety and judgment are the hallmarks of any truly skilled climber.

SELF-ARREST ON ICE

On ice, rather than rely on self-arresting to stop a fall, mountaineers usually choose to either solo and make a commitment not to fall or employ a rope system. There are, however, some ice conditions that fall somewhere in between snow and ice where there is some hope for arrest. In icy terrain, the self-arrest must be accomplished quickly, before speed is developed. If the climber is moving fast, crampons will stop the feet suddenly. Use the same general techniques as for self-arrest on snow, but realize that if a speeding climber touches crampons to the ice, they are likely to catch suddenly and turn an ankle or, worse, flip the climber over and send him or her tumbling down the ice. Some suggest that a fall on ice should be stopped only with the pick. Obviously, the stopping power of a self-arrest is significantly reduced without the use of the feet. Given this reduced effectiveness, be sure you'll be able to stop quickly. Better still, consider a belay.

STEP CUTTING

Step cutting was much more widely used before crampons became such effective tools. Mountaineers still cut occasional steps to cross small sections of ice where only a few steps will lead to easier terrain.

Cut steps in ice or hard snow with the adze or a couple of swipes with the pick of the ax. Use a long, fluid swing, and follow through rather than stick the ax in the ice. Make a final swipe with the adze to clear out the loosened ice. If you are faced with cutting more than a few steps, it will be faster to put on your crampons instead.

MOVEMENT AS A SAFETY SYSTEM

Climbing on ice that forms at a local crag can be a fairly casual and controlled experience. There are not often many objective hazards in such locales, and if weather threatens, home is not far away. These are the realms for testing and improving movement skills.

Wilderness mountaineering demands a different approach to movement. In remote terrain, objective hazards are both more prevalent and more difficult to predict. The lead climber may fall many feet before being caught by his or her rope, and the consequences of even fairly minor injuries when they occur miles from the nearest road can be severe. There will be times in the backcountry when your ability to judge terrain and move over it without falling becomes paramount.

In the beginning of this chapter I noted three components to movement as a safety system. There is a fourth. When faced with a situation in which you believe you might fall or you anticipate that the terrain is becoming too difficult, you must also be able and willing to down-climb to the last rest.

I have witnessed many climbers who moved up, found themselves on unsure ground, and then somewhat fearfully continued up farther into difficulty. Why they did not take that simple step back down to the pleasant holds they had only recently rested upon will forever be a mystery. If in a doubtful situation, climb back to a known position of safety and consider the situation thoroughly. Don't climb up into the unknown in search of easier ground that may not even exist.

Often after returning to a known rest or stance, you can compose a better route or prepare yourself more adequately for the difficult terrain to come. Sometimes you will choose to retreat altogether. Be prepared for these decisions; you will face them many times. From the beginning, accept the option of retreat.

Movement as a safety system as it applies to lead climbing is discussed in chapter 6.

4

Equipment

Travel through the mountains efficiently and safely. Assess the terrain, weigh your abilities, remain alert, and avoid objective hazards. Choose the route well so that the consequences of a misstep or broken foothold will not be great. Eventually, however, there will be a place where the consequences of a fall or error are greater—a place that is exposed and, though maybe not particularly difficult, still presents the possibility of a fall. All it takes is one unanticipated falling rock or a frantic bird scared out of its roost that flies into your face, and the consequences that seemed unlikely become real.

Most of us are willing to sacrifice a bit of purity for the sake of safety. We carry ropes and climb with partners to catch us if we fall. In mountains, desert canyons, or almost any remote terrain, it is not unlikely that you will confront some situation in which a rope would be useful. Rope systems are usually backups rather than aids to progress. They enable teams to climb more difficult and exposed terrain. The knowledge that you can be caught in the event of a fall calms the mind and body and allows you to focus on the problem at hand rather than dwell on horrid possibilities. Before learning the systems necessary to keep one another safe in steep terrain, you must learn how to handle rope and some other basic tools necessary to build a belay.

Much of the danger in mountaineering relates to the simple fact that it takes place in a steep environment. It is an environment where anything—be it a rock, a dropped piece of equipment, or a climber—accelerates if it is not held in place. Our primary safety system—the ability to climb and not fall—sometimes needs to be backed up in case it fails. The systems that accomplish this involve ropes.

ROPES

Ropes are designed to protect the climber from two basic forces: that of impact with the ground and that of being stopped too quickly. Only modern ropes are advanced enough to do both. Modern climbing ropes are dynamic. Their stretch absorbs a huge portion of the energy generated during falls—energy that would otherwise destroy weaker links in the safety system, such as a climber's body or even a carabiner. Somewhere between the steel cable and the bungee cord lies the modern climbing rope.

Ropes consist of a sheath woven around a core of twisted nylon fibers. The bulk of a rope's strength (over 80 percent) is built into the core. The sheath protects the fibers inside from abrasion, sun, and to some degree, water. With wear, a certain fuzziness develops as sheath fibers abrade. This is expected, and the fuzz becomes part of the protective qualities of the sheath. Up to 50 percent of the sheath fibers may break in various places along the rope before the sheath is truly worn.

All climbing ropes come with approval from the Union Internationale des Associations d'Alpinism (UIAA). Don't buy a rope that is not approved by the UIAA. The UIAA tests ropes to ensure that they are capable of holding some of the worst possible falls. On the ends of these ropes, there is a number, either 1 or $1/2$. A rope with 1 on its end is called a single rope and is considered safe for use by itself; a rope with a $1/2$ on its end is called a double rope and should be used in conjunction with another similar rope. The single ropes are larger in diameter and tested to higher capacities. The standard single rope is 9 to 11 millimeters in diameter and 50 meters long. The standard double rope is 8 to 9 millimeters in diameter and 50 meters long.

There are basically two ways to use ropes: with the anchor and belayer either above the climber or below. The first situation is called top roping, and the second, lead climbing. Figures 1 through 4 illustrate the kinds of falls ropes might hold.

Determining the actual energy that must be absorbed by the rope in each of the illustrated situations is a study in basic physics. Many of my students hated physics in school, but when they actually use it in a tangible manner, it is far more interesting. Perhaps you remember the following simple equation:

$$\text{energy of motion} = {}^{1}/_{2} \text{ mass} \times \text{velocity}^2$$

Therefore, the energy the rope must absorb when it stops a falling climber is equal to half the climber's weight times the square of the climber's speed at the moment the rope begins to stop the fall. Obviously the climber's weight does not change unless he eats a big meal during the fall. But as he falls, he accelerates, going faster each instant. The farther he falls, the faster he goes. There could be a great deal of energy generated in a long fall. Ropes disperse that energy over their entire available length.

Momentum equals mass multiplied by the speed of acceleration or deceleration. The forces on a stopping climber are related to how quickly that speed changes. Hit the ground, stop fast, and you're dead. A slow change in speed, like that supplied in belays with dynamic ropes, inflicts very little force on the climber.

In a top-roping situation, the length of the fall is always

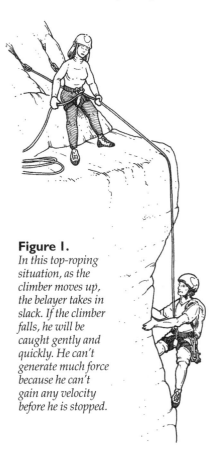

Figure 1.
In this top-roping situation, as the climber moves up, the belayer takes in slack. If the climber falls, he will be caught gently and quickly. He can't generate much force because he can't gain any velocity before he is stopped.

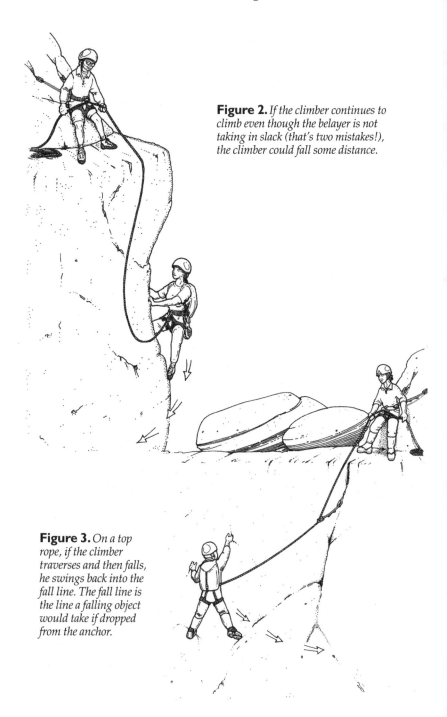

Figure 2. *If the climber continues to climb even though the belayer is not taking in slack (that's two mistakes!), the climber could fall some distance.*

Figure 3. *On a top rope, if the climber traverses and then falls, he swings back into the fall line. The fall line is the line a falling object would take if dropped from the anchor.*

less than the available length of rope. Dynamic ropes can absorb these energies quite easily.

Figures 1 through 4 illustrate four different possible falls. In figure 1, the climber can fall only the distance that the ropes can stretch plus the tiny amount of slack that might be in the system. He gets very little chance to pick up speed and hence generates very little energy. If the belayer is not vigilant and a loop of slack develops (figure 2), the climber can travel a much greater distance, accelerating all the way, and hence a great deal more energy must be absorbed by the rope.

If there is no slack in the rope but the climber moves off to one side, he will swing when he falls (figure 3). If it is solely a swinging fall, which we call a pendulum, the rope will have to hold a force of no more than twice the climber's body weight.

Now we come to the situations that inflict the greatest

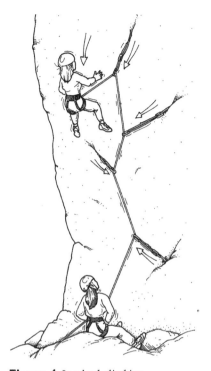

Figure 4. *In a lead-climbing situation, there is a potential for a much greater fall. Lead climbers generally place intermediate anchors through which the rope is run. If a lead climber fails to do this while climbing up from the belay ledge, there is the potential for falling a great distance before being caught.*

forces on our skinny little ropes: lead climbing or climbing above the belay. In figure 4, the leader has climbed up from a belay ledge. If she does not place any intermediate anchors and falls, she will fall the distance back to the ledge, plus that distance again below the ledge, plus some slack and stretch in the rope. She will fall more than twice the distance of available rope. In other words, she will fall a lot farther, gain far more speed, and then be stopped by only the same amount of rope as in figure 2.

Much greater energy must be absorbed in that same length of rope than in the very worst top-roping situation.

This, the worst possible fall in climbing, is given a fall factor of two. Simply put, a fall factor is the length of the fall divided by the length of available rope. Twenty feet of fall divided by only ten feet of available rope equals a fall factor of two—that's as bad as it gets. Ten feet of fall on ten feet of rope is a fall factor of one—not as bad, but still very significant. Falls of only a foot or two on many feet of rope are common in top-roping and lead-climbing situations; these create tiny fall factors that hardly affect the rope at all.

When we speak of energy being absorbed by a rope, we are really talking about the energy of motion being converted into other forms of energy. When a fall is held, kinetic energy is converted into heat, chemical changes in the nylon in the rope, actual broken strands of nylon in its sheath and core, and other energies that we hardly notice. Newton said it and it's still true: Energy is conserved even though it changes forms. All of these weaken the rope, and it must eventually be retired.

Every single rope tested for UIAA approval must be able to hold five factor two falls without failing. (The actual test fall is a 75-kilogram weight dropped 5 meters on 2.8 meters of rope, resulting in a fall factor of 1.78.) If a manufacturer advertises that a rope can hold more than five such falls, that is the manufacturer's determination and is not based on UIAA testing. A factor two fall is a huge event, and lead climbers take certain simple precautions to avoid them altogether. In fifteen years of climbing, I have been a party to only one factor two fall, and it was a harrowing experience.

IMPACT FORCE

UIAA-approved ropes have another number on the tag representing the maximum amount of force you, as the climber, could ever experience if you fall on that rope when it is new. Impact force is represented in pounds or kilograms. A low impact force means, generally, that the rope will absorb a great deal of energy in the process of stopping a falling climber. That means it will stretch a lot and take more time to stop the climber. Because the force a climber feels while stopping is linked to the time it takes to stop, a rope that stretches more means less force. A rope with a high impact force will stop you a bit more quickly.

ROPE CARE

Modern ropes do not "break" in mountaineering situations; they are cut, usually by sharp rock. Because of the weight and difficulty of handling multiple ropes, you will usually be protected by only one, so it is important that the rope, your only means of safety, be protected from cutting.

Your rope should always be protected from abrasion when in use, and since excessive falling weakens the rope, it is worth avoiding. Plus, you receive big style points for climbing a route without a falling. Acids and other chemicals, sunlight (ultraviolet radiation), and excessive heat all damage ropes and should be avoided. When not in use, the rope should be tucked away in a clean, dry bag. Dirt and grit work into the fibers of ropes and abrade them. Don't force particles into the rope by laying it in the dirt or by stepping on it. Wash ropes periodically by hand with a bit of mild, powdered detergent in water below 140 degrees Farenheit.

Age and environmental conditions compromise a rope's strength. Climbing ropes are made of nylon, which is 10 percent less strong with each passing year. At -45 degrees Farenheit, ropes are about 30 percent less strong. And when wet, nylon loses 10 to 20 percent of its strength and is far more elastic. Manufacturers offer a "dry" treatment, which helps ropes stay drier longer, adds a bit of durability to the sheath, and slows wear.

Abrasion and other forms of cutting are by far the biggest factors in compromising the strength of a rope. A rope with abraded spots, rockfall damage, or cuts of any kind should be retired.

ROPE HANDLING

It is difficult to climb faster than your comfort level or hike faster than your lungs and legs allow, but with practice you can shave hours off an ascent by handling the ropes quickly. Rope-handling efficiency may equal safety if lightning is striking nearby. Unexpected weather often arrives with little warning, so hours saved through efficient rope management can mean greater safety for your team. The time you earn will allow for more ambitious objectives.

Before learning how to handle the ropes, however, you need to know some basics, such as the difference between a bight and a loop. *(See illustration.)*

A bight (left) is an open bend in a rope, while a loop (right) is closed.

Stacking and Restacking

All or part of a rope not coiled or in use is called the stack. During a climb, managing that bit of extra rope effectively is an integral part of a team's efficiency. A stack should be a loose pile with both ends available. The end coming from the top of the pile is sometimes called the running or working end, or it can simply be called the top of the stack. Obviously, it is easier to pull rope off the top of the stack than from the bottom.

From a round coil, stack a rope by first throwing one end a few feet to the side of where you want your pile. This will leave it accessible after you're done. Then flake or toss loops one at a time into a neat pile, and leave the other end easily seen and off to one side. If your rope is in a butterfly coil, as described below, untie the hitch at the top, spread the bights apart, toss them onto the ground, and restack. Many people now use rope bags, which hold the rope in a neat stack and eliminate the need for coiling—another vanishing art.

If, for some reason, you want to use the end on the bottom, it is most efficient to restack the rope. To restack, take the top of the stack and toss it out to the side of the place you want your stack to lie. Run the rope through your hands, placing it in a neat pile. When you come to the other end, leave it easily in view off to one side of the stack.

The Butterfly Coil

A butterfly coil is made by placing a series of bights in your hand and then tying it all off with a hitch. This is a quick method because you start with both ends and coil a doubled rope.

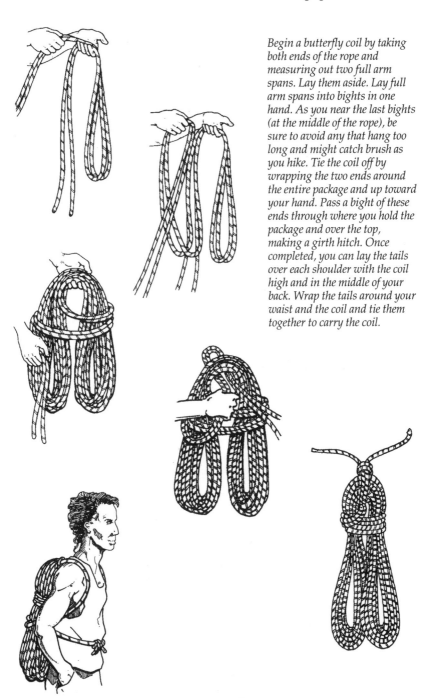

Begin a butterfly coil by taking both ends of the rope and measuring out two full arm spans. Lay them aside. Lay full arm spans into bights in one hand. As you near the last bights (at the middle of the rope), be sure to avoid any that hang too long and might catch brush as you hike. Tie the coil off by wrapping the two ends around the entire package and up toward your hand. Pass a bight of these ends through where you hold the package and over the top, making a girth hitch. Once completed, you can lay the tails over each shoulder with the coil high and in the middle of your back. Wrap the tails around your waist and the coil and tie them together to carry the coil.

Start with both ends of the rope and measure out two full arm lengths—a bit more if you are small. Letting that length hang free, take full arm-length bights of rope and lay them across your hand. Be sure you are laying bights, not loops, in your hand. When you've coiled the entire rope, even out the last few bights so that none are too short to be caught into the tie-off or so long that they will catch on bushes as you walk.

Now take the ends and wrap them from the middle of the bights back toward the top where you've been holding them. After three or four wraps, pass a bight of those ends through the coil and then back over the top. Pull the ends snug, and then use them to tie the coil onto your back if you wish.

Throwing a Rope

Look for simple solutions first. Sometimes you will be able to just lower an end of the rope down the face.

If you choose to throw the rope, be careful—people have been known to launch themselves off ledges while trying to throw down their ropes. The technique seems simple and obvious, but throwing a rope can be a trying experience on a windy day or in an awkward location. Avoid throwing a rope that is coiled in large loops, because these loops tend to tie themselves into knots en route.

Before doing anything, make sure one end of the rope is anchored and, if there is any possibility of falling, that the thrower is also anchored. Make bights in the rope. After about half the rope is in bights, set it aside or on your elbow, and make the rest of the rope into bights. Throw the bights made from the middle of the rope first, then throw the rest of the rope. Throwing the middle first adds some weight and speed when you throw the end.

OTHER TYPES OF CORDAGE

Many other lengths of accessory cord and webbing are used in rope systems to connect these systems to natural and artificial protection (discussed below). Whereas the dynamic climbing rope serves both as a connection between the climber and belayer and as a shock absorber, accessory cord and webbing usually serve only as connections and do not need to absorb energy like the rope. They are considered static because they stretch a relatively small amount. Many dynamic ropes, on the other hand, stretch as much as 50 percent longer before breaking.

A section of 7-millimeter accessory cord 3 meters long should be one of your first pieces of climbing gear. At first you can use this cordelette to practice knots and visualize techniques. Later, it will be useful in building anchors and performing rescue techniques.

Though most accessory cord and webbing is made of nylon and should be cared for in the same way as a rope, the fact that they need not be elastic allows manufacturers to use some different materials. One such material, called Kevlar, is more resistant to heat and stronger than nylon. It breaks down quickly when subjected to repeated bending, however, so though it is plenty strong, it would not be a good choice as a rappel line. Spectra is another fiber that is not elastic. In general, Spectra is stronger than nylon, is more resistant to abrasion, and holds up almost as well to bending abuse. When purchasing webbing or accessory cord, be sure to find out what it is made of and know any limitations to the use of that fiber.

Cordage	Tensile Strength
5mm Blue Water accessory cord	1,275 pounds
6mm Blue Water accessory cord	1,700 pounds
7mm Blue Water accessory cord	2,600 pounds
8mm Blue Water accessory cord	3,100 pounds
5.5mm Blue Water Spectra cord	4,500 pounds

Webbing	Tensile Strength
$9/16$-inch Blue Water Supertape	2,500 pounds
1-inch Blue Water tubular nylon	4,500 pounds
$9/16$-inch Blue Water Spectra sewn lining	4,500 pounds
$11/16$-inch Climb High Spectra sewn sling	5,500 pounds

Accessory cord from 5.5 millimeters in diameter is used to sling protection, which climbers use to attach their rope systems to cracks in the rock. Loop the cord through the piece, and tie the loop closed with a double fisherman's bend (see the section on knots later in this chapter). The loop provides a convenient place to add a carabiner and attach the rope. Because accessory cord is flexible, it also reduces the effect of the rope's motion on the security of an intermediate anchor. Steel wire is usually used to sling smaller wedges.

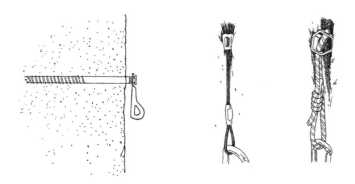

Rope teams attach themselves and their rope systems to the mountain with protection. Above are an ice screw, a wedge, and a passive cam.

Webbing is most commonly used to make loops called runners or slings. Slings are used either to extend the clip-in point of a piece of protection so that the rope can follow a better line or to connect several points of protection into an anchor. Webbing should have a tubular construction. Building anchors and placing protection call for slings of various lengths, from a very short runner (4 to 8 inches) called a quick draw to slings that fit over the shoulder. You can either buy the webbing by the foot and tie it into slings or purchase slings and quick draws that are sewn into loops. The sewn slings are strong and light but are difficult to tie around natural features.

CARABINERS

Also called "crabs," "biners," or "snap-links," carabiners were a major innovation in climbing equipment. Their invention allowed climbers to clip their ropes into anchor points rather than having to untie and thread the rope through or around the protection. Carabiners come in two basic varieties: locking and nonlocking.

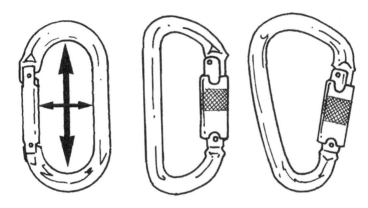

A regular oval carabiner, a D-shaped locking carabiner, and a pear-shaped locking carabiner.

Modern carabiners are very strong and are essential to safe, efficient rope systems, but they have limitations. When carabiners are used in a rope system, they can cause the system to fail in one of two ways: The rope may somehow come unclipped from the biner, or the biner may somehow be broken. Avoid the first hazard by either using locking biners (and remembering to lock them) or using two standard carabiners with their gates reversed. Better still is to both reverse and oppose the gates. Keep gates away from rock and other gear that might open them.

Two carabiners with gates reversed and opposed.

Carabiners are strongest in their long axis and with their gates closed. If a carabiner is loaded severely when the gate is open or in the wrong axis, it may break. There are carabiners on the market with very low "gate-open" strengths. In violent loading, carabiner gates have been shown to flutter open for a hundredth of a second or so. If a biner is loaded with more than its gate-open strength, it could break during this instant it is open. Try to avoid placing carabiners near rock edges that might open the gates when the rope comes taut. D-shaped carabiners direct the load to the spine side, away from the gate. Oval carabiners are a bit easier to handle and, when reversed, align nicely. Though ovals are versatile and my personal choice for general mountaineering, they are increasingly difficult to find as manufacturers meet the needs of ever more specialized climbers.

Bent gates are designed to make it easier to clip the rope to the biner with one hand. They should be used only between a quick draw or sling and the rope. For the most part, they are not versatile enough for use in the backcountry.

Several screw gate or locking biners have a place on every mountaineering rack. They are a bit heavier, usually stronger, and can be locked shut. This handy feature prevents accidental unclipping and gate-open loading.

HELMETS

Considering the possibility of falling rock or hitting one's head in a fall and the remoteness from medical facilities, I can think of few wilderness mountaineering situations in which I'd be happy without a hard hat. Buy a UIAA-approved climbing helmet that fits well with or without a hat, and wear it in steep terrain, especially if there is rockfall or icefall hazard.

HARNESSES

Because a harness distributes the force of a fall more evenly over a climber's body, it is more comfortable than tying into the rope directly with a bowline on a coil. As a result, choice, proper use, and conservative retirement of your harness are priorities.

Choosing a harness can be a daunting task—there are so many models available these days. The most important considerations are your climbing goals. Will you be traveling on glaciers or just cragging? Are you going to wear the harness all day long or just for short climbs? Define your goals, and then choose the harness accordingly.

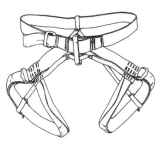

Learn to use that harness as it was designed to be used. Abide by the manufacturer's instructions. Your harness, along with the rope and the tie-in knot, is not backed up, so it deserves a high standard of use and care. Any harness should be retired if there is any doubt as to its integrity.

A climbing harness.

KNOTS

The climbing rope is one component of any system that often will not be backed up. Another is the tie-in knot. Knots are essential to mountain craft. Use your cordelette for practicing new knots and techniques. As you will see in later chapters, it should be carried on any climb involving rope work.

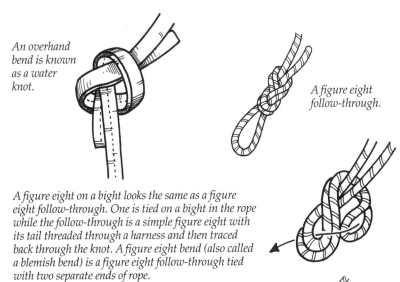

An overhand bend is known as a water knot.

A figure eight follow-through.

A figure eight on a bight looks the same as a figure eight follow-through. One is tied on a bight in the rope while the follow-through is a simple figure eight with its tail threaded through a harness and then traced back through the knot. A figure eight bend (also called a blemish bend) is a figure eight follow-through tied with two separate ends of rope.

The butterfly knot should be used instead of a figure eight on a bight when the bight and the two lines leaving the knot will be loaded in three separate directions.

Knots can be divided into three categories: knots, bends, and hitches. Knots are tied in the middle of a rope, bends tie two lines together, and hitches are tied around another object.

Bowlines should always be tied off with an overhand.

Tie a bowline on a coil to form an improvised swami belt if you do not have a harness.

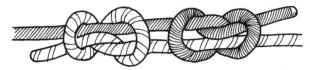

Use a double fisherman's bend to tie the ends of accessory cord together. It is a knot that is very difficult to untie.

When using a clove hitch, be sure the loaded line is on the spine side of the carabiner.

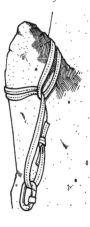

A girth hitch tied on a horn of rock.

The Münter hitch is useful as a source of friction in a belay but tends to twist the rope.

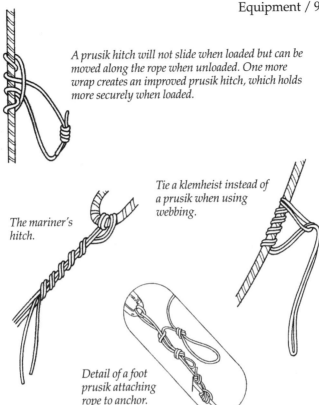

A prusik hitch will not slide when loaded but can be moved along the rope when unloaded. One more wrap creates an improved prusik hitch, which holds more securely when loaded.

Tie a klemheist instead of a prusik when using webbing.

The mariner's hitch.

Detail of a foot prusik attaching rope to anchor.

PROTECTION

Protection—or pro for short—refers to the gear that mountaineers use to attach their rope systems to the mountains. Protection can be divided into two categories: natural and artificial. A natural feature, such as a tree, boulder, or icicle, can be used as a point of protection by attaching slings to the feature and then attaching the slings to the rope. Climbers also carry an assortment of gadgets and devices to set in the rock, ice, or snow when the natural features are not enough. These are called artificial protection. Individual protection placements can be used as intermediate anchors or combined into belay anchors, which are explained in chapter 5.

The package of artificial protection and the slings, quick draws, and carabiners necessary to connect both artificial and natural pro to the rope is called a rack of gear. Considerations for preparing a rack of gear are in chapter 6.

When placing or evaluating any point of protection, consider the following:

1. Quality of the medium. Examine the quality of the vegetation, rock, ice, or snow and determine how strong it is and how well it is anchored to the terrain. Is it breakable rock? (Granite and quartzite, for example, are much stronger than sandstone and limestone.) Is the ice brittle?

2. Directionality. In what directions will the points of protection, either alone or connected together into an anchor, hold? What directions can the pro hold against and what directions of pull will cause it to weaken or fail?

3. Security. Will the artificial protection placements or the connections to natural features remain where you put them? A point of protection that falls out of place before you need it is not much good. Also consider whether it will be easy or difficult to remove.

4. Surface area. The amount of surface area in contact with the rock, ice, or snow is crucial to accurately evaluate protection placement.

Artificial pro like wedges and cams in solid rock will fail if they are in contact only with small crystals in the rock. An ice screw in contact with more air than ice is of little value. In general, a bigger piece of equipment will be stronger both in itself and because it has more contact with the medium.

NATURAL PROTECTION

Natural protection refers to any natural feature that might be used as a place to attach a rope system. Mountaineers must evaluate the feature's strength and attach the rope system securely and in the best place to minimize leverage.

Vegetation

Trees offer excellent points of protection, and larger ones can be used as belay anchors by themselves. Trees used as anchors should be alive and at least 6 inches in diameter. Also consider the depth of the soil in which the tree grows. Tie or girth-hitch slings around trees as near to the ground as possible to avoid unnecessary leverage on the tree. If you fear the sling will ride up on the tree, a girth hitch is best.

Bushes can be used in some situations, but they are far less secure than trees and should not be used alone.

Boulders

Boulders are commonly used in anchors, sometimes by themselves. Be conservative when evaluating boulders. There have been many stories of boulders thought to be secure that slid or rolled when loaded. The boulder should be large enough to counter the force a falling climber might generate and should lie on ground that is level or slopes away from the direction of force you anticipate. Sling or tie your rope around boulders low, preferably right at ground level.

Pinches

The point where two pieces of rock touch or two large boulders come together is called a pinch. As long as it is impossible for slings to work their way through pinches, they make excellent points of protection. Girth-hitch a sling around a pinch.

Pillars of Rock

For limited directions of pull, protrusions of rock can be girth-hitched. The rock must be solid, and the formation must lend itself to holding the sling until it is loaded. Pillars, which are called chicken heads when they stick out from a face, can be strong anchor points, but beware of your sling slipping off.

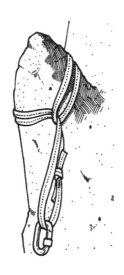

Chock Stones

Sometimes you will be lucky enough to find chock stones, rocks wedged in cracks. The chock stone and the surrounding rock must both be high-quality. They are usually good for limited directions of force. Be sure a sling girth-hitched around the chock stone will not rotate the stone and slip off.

Girth-hitch a sling to keep it in place on a pillar of rock.

Icicles

Some icicles can be slung. They must be several inches in diameter and well attached to ice above and below.

Threads

An ice rappel anchor can be made by using an ice screw to drill in the ice two holes that connect with one another. Remove the screw, and thread a piece of webbing through the passage with a wire hanger. Tie the ends of the webbing together with a water knot. In good ice, such anchors are extremely strong.

Make a passage to thread a sling in ice by drilling holes with an ice screw and pulling your sling through the hole with a wire hanger.

Bollards

Bollards are another sort of ice rappel anchor. Many climbers now use threads instead, but bollards still can be useful. Carefully chop a tear-shaped trench with your adze. Shape the upslope lip so that it will hold the rope as you rappel. You can put a sling around a bollard or put the rope directly around it. Bollards are very difficult to evaluate and time-consuming to build. Bollards can also be made in snow, but they must be large and are also very difficult to evaluate.

ARTIFICIAL PROTECTION

Climbers carry artificial protection to place in rock, ice, or snow when their natural protection is not enough. (See chapter 6 for information on racks.)

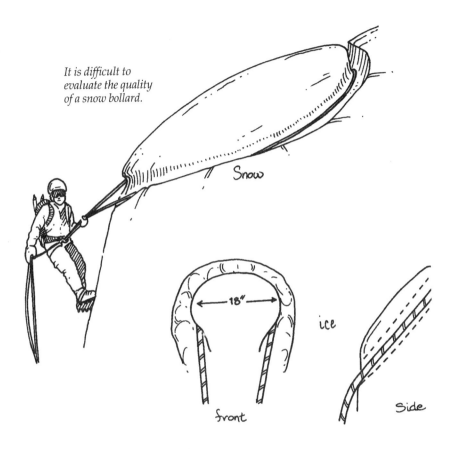

It is difficult to evaluate the quality of a snow bollard.

Snow

18"

ice

front

Side

On Rock

Rocks, especially strong intrusive igneous rocks, are a generally reliable medium. Well-placed chocks (bits of metal that wedge and cam in cracks) in good rock are very reliable. Protection is more questionable in softer sedimentary rocks like sandstone or in highly fractured rocks of any kind. Rock pro can be divided into hammerless (you can place it without a hammer) and hammered (you need a hammer to place it).

Hammerless Rock Protection. Most rock-climbing objectives can be protected with hammerless, or "clean," protection. Hammerless protection either wedges into a crack or cams

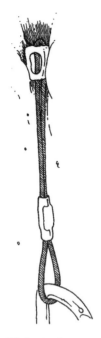

Wedge in place.

Hexcentric in place.

against the sides of a crack. Since such protection usually does not scar the rock at all and is easy to place and remove, it is best to "climb clean" if the route will allow it.

Wedges are simple chocks that can be slotted into cracks above narrower sections. When pulled toward the narrower portion of the crack, they wedge against the rock. Examples of wedges are Black Diamond Stoppers and Wild Country Rocks. In Eastern Europe, some climbers even use knots. Look for places where you can fit the wedge into the crack, and slot it down into a place where it cannot escape. Wedges hold forces in a limited number of directions. The surface area of contact with the rock should be maximized. All other considerations being equal, a larger wedge is a stronger placement.

Some wedges are spring-loaded. When placed in a crack and pulled upon, the two parts of the piece slide along one another. The greater the pull, the more the piece widens and exerts force on the rock. They are very effective in small, parallel-sided cracks but are sometimes difficult to remove.

Cams rotate into a wider orientation when you pull on them and hence multiply the force they receive onto the rock in which they are placed. They are very secure when placed well.

Passive cams without springs are lightweight but versatile protection. They should be placed above narrower portions of a crack. Though the narrowing does not have to be as pronounced as that needed for a wedge, passive cams will not stay in place in a parallel crack. The first passive camming device was the Great Pacific Iron Works Hexcentric. The hexcentric is still a simple and effective piece, often better than active cams in soft sandstone.

Chock size		Side width (mm)	Edge width (mm)	Weight (gm)	Side strength (kN)	Edge strength (kN)
0	Wild Country Rock	4.4	9.6	6	2	2
$1/4$	Wild Country Rock	4.9	10.6	6	2	2
$1/2$	Wild Country Rock	5.6	11.6	10	2	2
$3/4$	Wild Country Rock	6.9	12.1	10	2	2
1	Wild Country Rock	7.0	13.0	16	7	4
2	Wild Country Rock	8.2	13.8	25	12	4
3	Wild Country Rock	9.6	14.5	28	12	6
4	Wild Country Rock	11.3	15.3	30	12	8
5	Wild Country Rock	13.3	16.8	32	12	8
6	Wild Country Rock	15.6	19.0	36	12	10
7	Wild Country Rock	18.4	21.2	38	12	12
8	Wild Country Rock	21.6	24.0	47	12	12
9	Wild Country Rock	24.4	27.7	60	12	12
10	Wild Country Rock	30.0	31.0	71	12	12

Lowe Tri-cams are another lightweight and effective passive camming device. Some are shown on the rock rack in the figure on page 140.

Active cams are spring-loaded, which gives them a huge advantage. The springs add security by holding the cams in position until they are loaded. As a result, spring-loaded camming devices (SLCDs) can be placed in parallel-sided or even slightly

Friend in place.

flaring cracks. The strongest SLCDs have four cams, two on each side of a shaft or wire. The first SLCD was the Wild Country Friend, a breakthrough for climbers in the late 1970s. It has a rigid shaft. Beware of levering this shaft over an edge or narrowing in a crack. Camalots, Flexible Friends, and three-cammed units (TCUs) all have flexible wire shafts.

All SLCDs should be placed with their cams in the middle of their range. Cams that are forced into the smallest range are difficult to remove; those that are extended into the largest range are less secure and tend to "walk" into different placements.

SLCD		Expansion range (mm)	Weight (gm)	Strength (kN)	Cam stop strength (kN)
1.0	Wild Country Friend	19–29	89	14	11
1.25	Wild Country Friend	21–33	94	14	11
1.5	Wild Country Friend	23–35	94	14	12
1.75	Wild Country Friend	25–41	100	14	12
2.0	Wild Country Friend	29–44	106	14	12
2.5	Wild Country Friend	33–55	120	14	12
3.0	Wild Country Friend	43–66	143	14	13
3.5	Wild Country Friend	51–82	168	14	13
4.0	Wild Country Friend	64–100	216	14	14

Friend is a registered trademark of Wild Country

Hammered Rock Protection. Many sorts of rock protection must be placed with a hammer. Most climbs, however, do not require hammered protection. Since all hammered protection damages the rock to some degree, employing it is a serious decision. Two types that you will likely encounter on rock are pitons and bolts.

Pitons are metal wedges or angles driven into cracks in the rock. They range in size from narrow wedges that can be driven into the thinnest cracks to very wide pitons called bongs that fill cracks 4 inches wide. Pitons larger than about 1 inch wide have mostly been replaced by camming devices.

Pitons are still widely used on aid climbs and in remote mountains. They are very secure when well placed. Choose a piton that fits about halfway into the crack you want to use, and hammer it in. As the piton becomes more secure, the ring of each hammer blow becomes audibly higher. Dull sounds indicate loose rock and a poor placement. Use a hammer to check the quality of preexisting, or "fixed," pitons. You should hear the high-pitched ring of a well-placed pin.

Bolts are driven into holes that are drilled in the rock. The drill is usually a chisel-type drill rotated by hand while being hit by a hammer. The hole is permanent. Bolts are very difficult to evaluate once they have been placed. There is no way of knowing for sure if the bolt is 1 inch deep or 3 inches deep. The diameter of the bolt, however, can be ascertained by looking at the head.

In the backcountry, most bolts are placed by hand and are $1/4$ or $3/8$ inch in diameter and between 1 and 2 inches long. The bolt hanger, to which you clip your carabiner, should be flush and snug against the rock. It should not spin around the bolt. The bolt itself should be driven into its head and unmovable.

On Ice

Ice is a far less reliable medium than rock. Placements lose strength as the sun shines upon them or as they slowly melt under the pressure of a load.

Ice screws are screwed into the ice. They are hollow so the ice that is displaced by the screw can exit through the hollow center. Seventeen-centimeter Black Diamond ice screws sunk to the eye in good ice are rated by the manufacturer to hold 4,040 pounds. The question is, what is good ice? Look for ice that is dense and blue rather than white and filled with air. In general, concavities in the ice are stronger, though it is sometimes awkward to rotate a screw in a deep concavity. Clear away weak or questionable ice before placing your screw. A small pilot hole made with the pick of your ax will help you start the screw.

Ice pitons, especially the Lowe Snargs, were for many years the easiest ice protection to place. Sharp, thin-walled modern screws are slowly changing that, however.

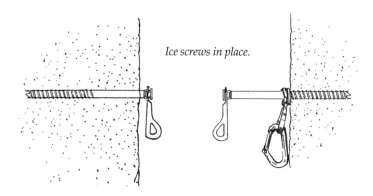

Ice screws in place.

Ice pitons are driven into the ice with a hammer. Clear away rotten surface ice before placing an ice piton. Remove the piton by unscrewing.

On Snow

Snow is the most difficult to evaluate of all the mediums. Often, snow protection and anchors are so hard to evaluate that mountaineers dig holes in the snow for belays that rely mostly on the belayer's position. Snow protection can either be buried—a dead man—or be driven in, or picketed.

Almost anything can be used as a dead man: Ice axes, packs, and shovels all have been slung and buried as dead man anchors. Whatever you use, the dead man should be slung at the center of its surface area. Dig a hole without disturbing the snow

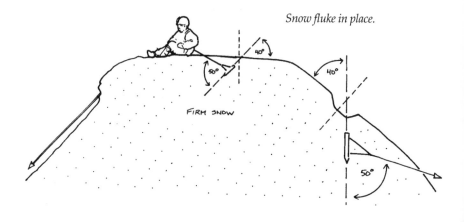

Snow fluke in place.

FIRM SNOW

in the downslope direction, and bury the slung item. Make a path for the sling in the direction in which you anticipate the force. A piece of protection specifically designed as a dead man is called a snow fluke.

An ice ax or a snow stake can be driven into the snow, or picketed, at an angle of 30 to 40 degrees away from the direction of force. Pickets are valuable only if the snow is hard and the picket is difficult to drive. If a picket is easily driven, opt for burying it as a dead man.

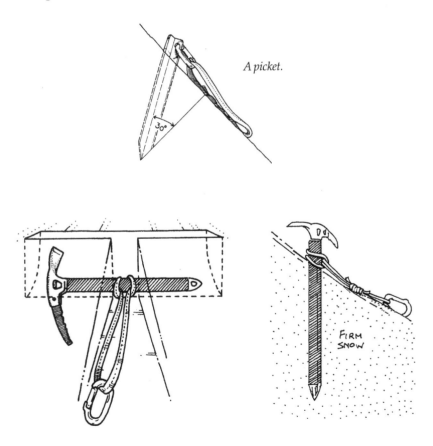

A picket.

FIRM SNOW

An ice ax used as a picket (right) and buried as a dead man (left).

TYING IN

The most basic way to attach yourself to the rope is to tie it directly to your body with the bowline on a coil. This technique is simple, uses no extra equipment, and is useful for those times you may be without a harness. It is, however, uncomfortable and even dangerous in more than a very short fall. It also uses up several feet of rope that you may need for another purpose.

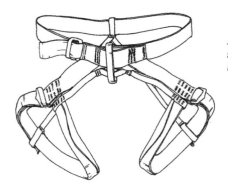

Always check to make sure your harness is buckled correctly.

It is far more common to wear a harness and tie the rope directly to that harness with a figure-eight follow-through. When putting on a harness or tying a knot, never allow yourself to be interrupted. Focus and concentrate on the procedure. There have been too many incidents in which a climber, interrupted during one of these crucial procedures, has failed to finish a knot or double the tail back through a buckle. As you can imagine, the consequences are dire. At NOLS we often use the following three-point check procedure to ensure that a climber and his or her partner are in the system safely:

1. Is your harness on correctly and buckled or tied correctly?
2. Is your knot tied correctly through both waist and leg loops, and is it dressed with adequate tail?
3. Is your belayer in the system correctly and ready to belay?

The importance of checking a tie-in procedure cannot be overemphasized. Many aspects of rope systems are redundant and backed up in case one part fails. Your harness, the tie-in knot, your belayer, and the rope itself are not backed up, so check them frequently and carefully.

5

Safety Systems

Judge the terrain in front of you, choose the best route, and determine whether you can travel over it. Route finding, hazard evaluation, and movement skills make up a mountaineer's first lines of defense. As the likelihood or the consequences of a slip or fall increase, the climber is faced with two options: either go an easier way or use a rope system to catch a possible fall.

Even when the likelihood of a fall seems very low, prudence demands some form of backup. Falls can be unexpected and are often caused by unforeseen events such as a hold that breaks, a slippery rock, or a rosy finch flying in the climber's face.

BELAYS

On the tall sailing ships, sailors controlled huge sails without the aid of winches by wrapping their lines around wooden spikes known as belay pins. The friction of the rope around the pins allowed the sailors to manage huge forces. Climbers use similar techniques to handle the forces of a falling climber and have adopted the term belay. Belay means to secure the climber with the rope and also refers to the place chosen for belaying and to the entire system including the belayer, the climber, and the equipment that holds them to the mountain.

Belays can be simple, like plunging an ice ax into the snow to anchor yourself on a slope, or complicated. Either way, when one team member says, "On belay," she promises to safeguard and manage her partner's lifeline indefinitely. Fulfilling the roles of belayer, supporter, and potential rescuer, a belayer's responsibility does not end until her partner says, "Belay off."

Any belay, no matter what its form, is made up of four components that must be considered when you build or evaluate any rope system: friction, position, anchor, and communication.

The climber being backed up by the belay is moving, so the belay must be adjustable. Simply passing the rope through your hands allows the freedom to adjust the rope length, but the friction produced in holding the climber in the event of a fall would burn your hands. Friction transforms the force created by a fall into heat and other energy. A hip belay, in which the rope is wrapped once around the waist, is a simple way to add enough friction to stop short falls; for longer falls, you will need to use some sort of simple device. When initiating any belay, ask yourself, "Is there enough friction in the system for me to hold the worst possible fall?"

Another part of a good belay is the belayer's position with respect to the climber and the direction from which the pull will come. Belayers should orient their bodies to face the anticipated force and choose a stance that helps them brace against it. A deep hole on a snow slope can offer secure position. Secure position is more difficult to find on steep rock, but there will usually be a protrusion behind which you can brace yourself.

The ultimate backup to the belay is the anchor. It holds the belayer or the team to the mountain no matter how bad the fall. Evaluate position and anchor together, in relation to one another. One's position should take as much of the force as possible in order to protect the anchor from being compromised. In some situations, such as in soft snow, you will find excellent position and can afford to rely less on an anchor. At other times, as in a hanging belay, you have little or no position, and the anchor must hold the full force of both the belayer and the falling climber. When evaluating the anchor and belayer position, consider the worst possible load that could come onto the belayer and the directions it might come from, the belayer's position, and the quality of the anchor.

The final component of the belay is communication. It may seem less essential than friction, position, and anchor, but it is far more crucial than many realize. Effective communication makes for a smooth and effficient team. Ineffective communication not only slows a team but also can result in excessive slack or tension in the rope. You will observe people who hardly speak to one another during their climb; they are communicating nonetheless. Likely they have been partners for years and know, almost in advance, each other's needs. When you are new to this game, climbing with a new partner, or when conditions make words difficult to understand, a precise, predetermined signal system is essential.

These four elements—friction, position, anchor, and communication—represent our effort to stop a falling climber. In the vertical world, gravity is always there, holding you on the rock, pulling you toward the earth, and accelerating you if you fall. It is this acceleration of the falling climber that results in vast amounts of energy that the belay must absorb or dissipate when we hold or catch a fall.

The stretch of the rope, along with friction over terrain and through belay devices, dissipates that energy and makes the force of a fall easier to control. The anchor counters the force and keeps the whole system from failing. Position helps counter the force, protecting the anchor. Communication ensures the coordination of the belay.

The most difficult terrain people climb without using artificial aids for progress is Class 5. Climbers employ some of the same terminology used in rating climbs to identify various rope techniques. The technique generally used for 5th Class terrain is aptly called the 5th Class belay. Because 5th Class terrain is the most difficult—falls are likely, consequences are high—the 5th Class belay offers maximum security. It is also one of the most time-consuming techniques, because only one team member moves at a time while the other manages the rope. The British sometimes refer to it as climbing singly.

A TYPICAL 5TH CLASS CLIMB

The rope, in this case a 50-meter-by-10-millimeter dynamic, is stacked neatly at the base of the climb. The lead climber ties into the top of the stack. The follower, or second, ties into the end at the bottom of the stack. Then the second ties herself to an anchor near the base of the climb and sits in good position for an upward pull. The second takes rope from near the leader and places it into an appropriate friction device. After they check one another, the second—the belayer—says, "On belay," and the climb begins.

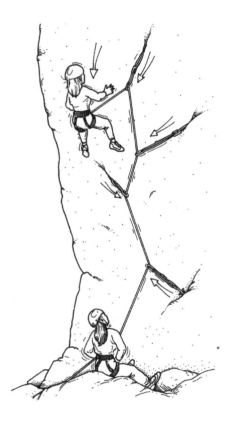

Belayers pay out or take up rope in response to the needs of climbers, sometimes responding to verbal signals from climbers, but mostly just feeling and seeing the needs and meeting them. As climbers make progress up the pitch—the distance traveled between two belay anchors or stations—they place intermediate anchors (discussed in chapter 4) to reduce the length of possible falls and to protect the most difficult moves.

Climbers place these intermediate anchors for many reasons. Paramount is that the protection be placed so that it catches a falling climber before she hits the ground or a ledge. Obviously, if climbers are near the ground, the protection must be spaced more closely, because even a short fall would put the climber on the deck.

Leading out. *When leading, the lead climber is above the belay. If he falls, he will fall twice the distance to the last intermediate anchor plus the stretch of the rope.*

Once a lead climber, nearing the end of the rope, reaches a good place to anchor, she builds an anchor, ties into it, and calls, "Belay off," to the second. The leader then belays as the second climbs up the same pitch. The second is protected by a top-rope belay, in which the rope is above, kept taut by the leader, who is always ready to catch a fall. During the climb, the second removes any intermediate anchors the leader placed for protection so that they can be used again on future pitches.

Generally, the second remains on belay at the ledge and, after reorganizing the gear, becomes the leader for the next pitch. This technique, called swinging leads, allows both climbers to share the leading and benefit from the mental rest of following half the time. One pitch at a time, each climbing in turn, the team makes progress up the mountain.

A CLOSER LOOK AT THE HIP BELAY

For much of mountaineering's history, the hip belay, or a variation of it, was the only 5th Class belay technique. It can be created with just a rope and two people. Advances in equipment and technique have sent the hip belay reeling toward extinction, but it continues to have a deserved place in a mountaineer's bag of tricks. This is primarily because it is simple and quick and in many situations adequate to control a fall.

Let's examine such a situation closely. Imagine a climber with a rope at the top of a crag. Another climber is at the bottom. The climber at the bottom wants to get to the top but wants to be safeguarded in case of a fall. The climber at the top throws an end of the rope to the climber, who ties into it. What next? Let's look at the basic hip belay in terms of the four components: friction, position, anchor, and communication.

FRICTION

The belayer pulls up rope until she feels the climber, who says, "Zero!" or "That's me!" indicating that there is no more rope to pull up. As the climber begins to make progress, the belayer could simply pull up rope, hand over hand. But could she hold him if he fell? Not likely; she must be sure the belay will hold.

She needs to add friction to the system so that she will be able to hold the weight of her partner easily.

By passing the rope around her body just above the hips and to a brake hand, she adds enough friction to hold her partner's weight with ease. The brake hand always grasps the rope, no matter what. The guide hand—on the rope that goes directly to the climber—helps manage the rope and is also free for other tasks.

As her partner climbs nearer, she must take up slack without ever letting her brake hand leave the rope. Starting with her brake hand near the hip and guide hand reaching down the climber's rope, she slips rope around her body to take in slack. She then slaps her guide hand out in front of the brake and grabs both ropes while she slides her brake hand back to her hip. Now she is in position to slip, slap, slide again to take in another bit of rope.

If the second wants to climb back away a few moves, the belayer simply feeds the rope out with her guide hand while letting it slide through her brake hand. This motion must become second nature and ambidextrous. With practice, like riding a bicycle, your body will slip, slap, and slide naturally and without error.

During this process, your brake hand should always be ready to wrap the rope more completely around your body in the event of a fall. Don't let it get too far out in front of you or to the side. Most important, never let it get behind your hip.

The belay motion is the same when using a belay device. Make it smooth by moving your brake and guide hands along parallel lines, and remember that you brake a belay device by pulling back on the rope.

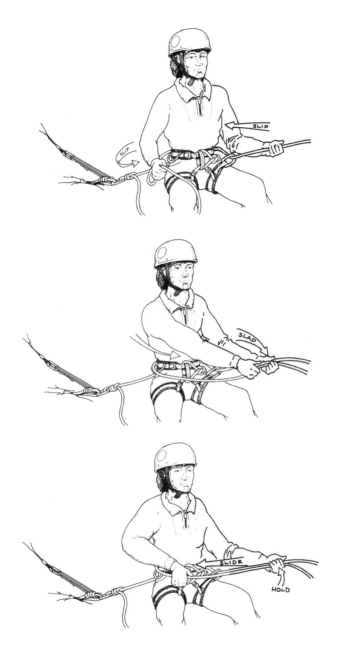

Taking in slack with the hip belay is a three-part motion. Starting with your guide hand outstretched and your brake hand just in front of your hip, slip rope around your back (a), slap your guide hand out again and grasp both ropes beyond your brake hand (b), and slide your brake hand back into position near your hip (c). Say the words as you learn, and be ready to brake the rope (brake hand across your body) in the event of a fall.

POSITION

We use our body position to hold as much force as we can so we don't rely solely on the anchor. But you can expect some pretty big forces in most climbing situations, and in almost every fall at least some of the load comes onto the anchor. The belayer should sit so that the rope from her waist to the anchor is taut and in line with the anticipated direction of pull. This way the belayer will not be pulled out of position and then stopped by the anchor with a sudden jerk. Good position avoids both a painful ride across the ledge and unnecessary force on the anchor caused by a few feet of extra acceleration.

Routes often traverse, and the direction of force is hard to predict. Diverging too much from the direct line up the crag may have consequences. A fall will cause the climber to swing quite a distance until back on the plumb line down from the anchor. Also, the load may come from an unexpected direction, which could pull the belayer out of position, loading the anchor unnecessarily.

When a climber falls or pulls on the rope in a hip belay, the force comes onto the belayer's body, mostly on the guide side. This tends to twirl the belayer out of position, which could cause the belay to fail. If the anchor line is on the guide side and taut as it should be, it will counter such a twirl. Further ensure that the rope stays where it should by clipping it through a carabiner, or

In snow, mountaineers can often get excellent belayer position.

guide biner, on that side. This will keep the rope from being pulled under the body or over the head.

When the hip belay is set up correctly, with the anchor line and a guide biner both on the guide hand side, the rope goes from the climber to the biner, round the back, and to the stack. It is very important that the foot and leg the belayer braces with are on the same side as the rope going out to the climber. The leg brace will thus be on the side opposite the brace hand.

ANCHOR

Building an anchor can be a complicated procedure or as simple as girth-hitching slings around a large tree. Anchors are the last line of defense. They must not fail.

Anchors come in all sizes and designs. Build them with the anticipated use, directions of pull, and worst possible scenarios in mind. The uses for anchors include top-rope anchors, bottom anchors for lead climbs, and anchors on belay ledges that serve as both bottom and top-rope anchors. Each of these anchors must be multidirectional, or capable of holding forces from many different directions.

Think of a top-roping situation. It is often convenient on shorter crags to have the rope slung in "yo-yo" fashion, with the rope going from the climber up to the anchor, where it runs through biners, and then down to the belayer. The belayer may also have an anchor to keep from being lifted off the ground. In this situation, the belayer can see the climber, and there should not be any slack in the system. A falling climber will be caught immediately and will load the rope with little more than body weight, say 120 pounds. The belayer, to stop the fall, must counter that force with 120 pounds. So the load that is actually "felt" by the yo-yo anchor is twice that of the falling climber. Convenience is the advantage of this situation, but the pulley system it creates at the anchor doubles the force it must hold, so build a good anchor. For best position in a yo-yo scenario, place gravity on your side by standing as close as possible to directly below the top anchor without being in undue rockfall danger. For climbers of similar weight, this position is adequate to counter a fall. If the climber is heavier, the belayers will need anchors to hold them to the ground.

When building anchors on belay ledges for a second climber, the belayer has the advantage of position in the system, and there is no pulley acting on the anchor. Loads may be very small. But that same anchor will be used to belay a lead above it. If the

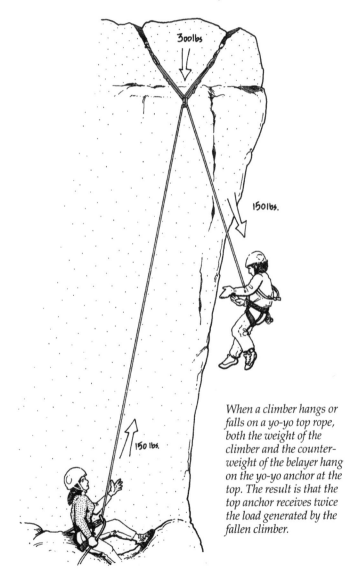

When a climber hangs or falls on a yo-yo top rope, both the weight of the climber and the counterweight of the belayer hang on the yo-yo anchor at the top. The result is that the top anchor receives twice the load generated by the fallen climber.

leader were to fall before placing the first piece of protection, accelerating for many feet before being caught by that anchor, the anchor would face forces equivalent to thousands of pounds.

Use the acronym SRENE to remember this simple outline of considerations each time you build an anchor:

> **S**ound protection placement
> **R**edundancy
> **E**qualize
> **N**o **E**xtension

Sound Protection Placement

Belay anchors depend on sound protection placements. When placing each piece in an anchor, consider the quality of the rock, ice, snow, or vegetation; the directions in which the piece can be loaded; the contact between the piece and the medium; and whether the protection will stay in place.

Redundancy

Most belay anchors are also backed up, or redundant. Thus if any single component of an anchor fails, it will not cause complete failure of the anchor. Anchors are built with protection points plus the slings and biners that connect them. If any sling comes untied, biner opens, or piece pulls out, the anchor should still hold. As one of my climbing partners says, "If an anchor fails, there are no excuses!"

Redundancy protects us against equipment failure, an unexpectedly weak medium, and most important, human error. Our own mistakes are by far our greatest nemesis. It is difficult to evaluate the rock quality correctly every time. So back that decision up—place another piece. Water knots can loosen; check them or add another sling. What is the necessary level of redundancy in an anchor? In determining what needs to be redundant, consider the amount of gear you have, the likelihood of a component's failure, and the level of attention you will give it while in use.

There are parts of anchors where redundancy is not necessary. For example, mountaineers don't usually carry enough gear to back up each locking biner. But since it isn't backed up, it is a good idea to check it frequently to make sure the gate is still locked. The harness, the rope, and the tie-in knot are usually not backed up. Because they are not redundant, it is necessary to give them special consideration and check them thoroughly and frequently. If there are components in the anchor that you choose not to make redundant, they should be ones that are not crucial to the anchor's integrity and that you can check often, or you should be very sure that they will not fail.

Equalize

The third consideration in building anchors is how much the load is equalized among the anchor points. It often makes sense for the various points in an anchor to share the load rather than

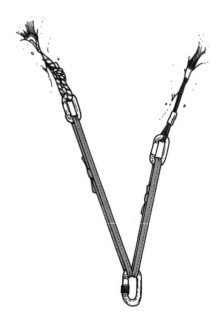

to have one point hold all the load with others as unloaded backups. Use some of the following construction techniques to build equalized anchors.

Nonadjustable Anchors. One way to distribute a load evenly among several anchor points is to tie them together in such a way that all connecting points are taut when the anchor is loaded. If the direction of pull changes, however, this system will not adjust, and one anchor point will take more than its share.

Separate pieces are independent systems right down to their connecting point at a locking biner. If one fails, the other remains intact. If you leave the anchor unattended, as with a yo-yo top rope, consider also

In this anchor, two pieces are connected together with separate slings. The slings are sized correctly to distribute the force evenly between the pieces in one plane of direction.

making the locker redundant by adding another regular biner.

In most situations, all it takes is a bit of thought for the anchor builder to determine the direction of force accurately. Positioning pieces to share the load in that direction of force is an excellent way to build most anchors, because each piece can be its own separate system.

Self-adjusting Systems. If the load could come from many different directions, consider making it a self-equalizing anchor. A self-equalizing system could be created by simply running both strands of a sling through the central locking carabiner. As the load moves around, the biner slides back and forth, self-adjusting to pulls from different directions. The disadvantage is that if one piece were to fail, it could slip through that locking

Tying in to an anchor using rope saves slings and is quick. Here the climber has anchored to three pieces by tying a figure eight on a bight and two clove hitches. It is especially effective when there are only one or two anticipated directions of force and a team is swinging leads.

biner, causing the entire system to fail. A twist in one side of the sling, known as the magic X, will prevent a failed piece from slipping through the locking biner.

Note that if left as it is, this system is not completely redundant. The magic X prevents the sling from pulling through the locking biner in the event that one piece fails, but nothing is backing up the sling itself. A loose knot would mean total failure for the anchor.

No Extension

One problem with many self-equalizing systems is that if one piece fails, the anchor elongates as the load comes onto the other piece. This extension allows for unwanted acceleration and a

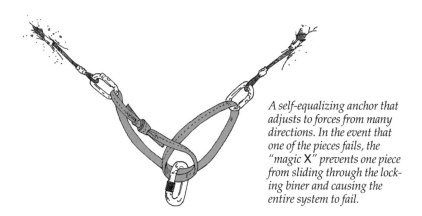

A self-equalizing anchor that adjusts to forces from many directions. In the event that one of the pieces fails, the "magic X" prevents one piece from sliding through the locking biner and causing the entire system to fail.

jarring stop in the event of a fall. As a result, such a system should be used only as a single element in a larger anchor. Non-adjustable anchors eliminate the possibility of extension if one portion fails. While you may incorporate self-equalizing features into an anchor, limiting extension and adding redundancy are more important considerations when building an anchor.

Other Considerations

Pieces Placed in Opposition. Since multipitch belay anchors must hold pulls from many directions, they often include individual pieces to hold pulls in opposing directions. If pieces are in horizontal cracks, they may hold well for both upward and

Tie a locking girth hitch as shown.

downward pulls. If the cracks are vertical, an upward pull is likely to pull them out of the rock. One interesting trick that helps make a belay anchor more multidirectional is the locking girth hitch.

A locking girth hitch adds security to an anchor by ensuring that the piece on which the hitch is tied won't receive a pull from a direction that might pull it out. The hitch also creates a small amount of tension between the two pieces and helps hold less secure protection in place. Sometimes the locking girth hitch is helpful in keeping stopper placements in horizontal cracks, where they might otherwise wiggle out from rope drag. Pieces can also be held in opposition but locked in place with the mild tension offered in the locking girth hitch, with a carabiner, quick draw, or sling.

It may look as if the locking girth hitch creates a pulley system that increases the load on the piece the hitch is tied upon. This is true, but the increased load is negated by the substantial friction in the hitch. A more important consideration when using the locking girth hitch, and in anchor building in general, is the various angles in the anchor and how they affect the loads on individual protection placements.

Angles and forces. Whereas equalization evens the force on each piece, changing the direction of the force as it moves through the anchor can multiply small loads into excessive force. Note in the accompanying figure how the loads on each piece vary with the angle. Imagine an angle of 180 degrees. It should seem clear that pulling on the locking biner will produce a greater force at each piece.

Keep the angles in your anchors below 90 degrees and certainly below 120 degrees. Keeping the angles small results in less force being transferred to the individual pieces. If you keep placements relatively close together, it will be easier to keep the angles small, use less webbing to connect them together, and reduce the shock-load potential in the basic magic X self-equalizing system.

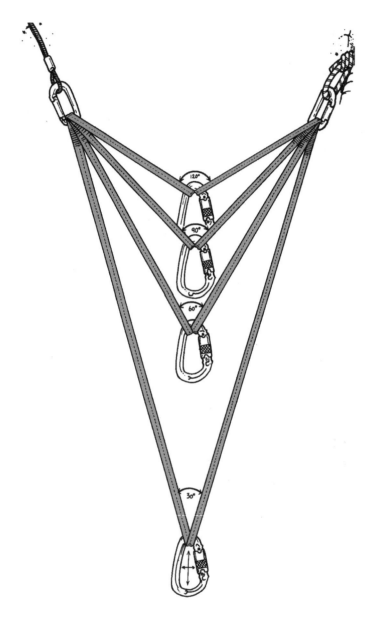

The forces on individual placements increase as the angle at the connection point widens from half the load on each anchor with an angle of 0 to the equivalent of the entire load on each anchor at 120.

COMMUNICATION

Over the roar of a nearby river or a loud wind, even the simplest words can become difficult to understand. In such situations, stick to a predetermined signal system. The best system varies the number of syllables in each word to differentiate signals in noisy conditions. It does not matter so much what system of signals you choose, but it should be useful and understandable in all conditions.

Two-syllable signals shouted by the climber mean essentially the same thing. "Climbing," "Up rope," "Falling," and the infrequently used "Tension" all mean "Hold me!" They are the climber's request for security.

To reduce confusion, all signals should receive a response. Even if the belayer is slow to accomplish a task, a "Thank you" reassures the climber that the signal was heard.

Some signals are differentiated by cadence rather than the number of syllables. "Belay . . . off" has a different cadence than "On . . . belay." Here, the cadence should be emphasized.

"Rock!" and "Slack" both have one syllable. To differentiate, "Rock!" should be shouted urgently and then repeated. Those who hear "Rock!" should not take the time to respond—they must immediately dodge the hazard.

There are situations in which even a very accurate system cannot be understood over the wind or the roar of a nearby river. At such times, it is important to be able to read what the leader is doing through the movement of the rope. Generally, signals are not as important during the pitch as at the beginning and end of the pitch. If attentive, you will learn to feel exactly what a climber is doing through the rope. There will be lots of rope movement during a pitch, punctuated by pauses for protection placements, route finding, or rest. At the end, there is usually a longer pause while the climber builds the next belay anchor, then quicker rope movement as slack is pulled up. Then there are sharp tugs as the climber above puts the second on belay. It is important that this last act is very clear. Three sharp tugs on the rope make a clear rope signal for "On belay."

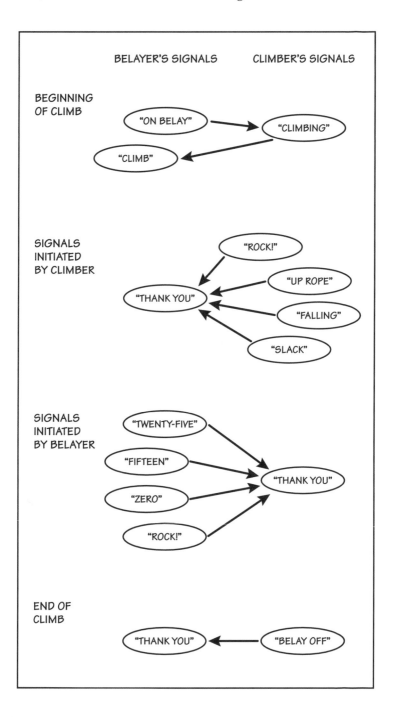

ROPE SYSTEMS: A PROGRESSION

The various belay techniques one might employ in the mountains are often treated as different systems. In reality, each system—be it a running belay, a fixed line, or a 5th Class belay—is a variation on the same theme. Each climbing situation demands a different combination of friction, position, anchor, and communication to satisfy the needs for security while allowing for adequate speed. There is, then, a continuum or progression of rope systems.

Keeping the four elements of a belay in mind, let's look at this progression beginning with the fastest and least secure and ending with those that sacrifice speed to increase security.

FREE SOLOING

Free soloing—no rope, just you and your ability and judgment. The word evokes images of reckless rock stars high off the ground, but soloing is a part of every mountaineering day. Everybody solos within his or her own personal comfort level, and it is important to know that limit and to understand soloing as a technique that has limitations but that can be done safely. Soloing allows the climber to cover terrain quickly but offers little room for errors in judgment, climbing mistakes, or unexpected objective hazard.

Think of a situation in which soloing might be most appropriate. It should be a situation in which either the likelihood or the consequences of a fall are negligible. If you are climbing up a pure snow slope that slowly levels off to flat snow at its base, and you fall, the worst consequence is probably that you would slide to the bottom and slowly stop as the slope levels off. Maybe you are on the broad summit ridge of a peak and, although the ridge drops off steeply on either side, to fall over the edge would require an effort. In either of these examples, a rope system would only slow you down.

These examples are fairly straightforward. As you confront more difficult decisions, remember that the wilderness does not forgive errors: Always consider your level of protection. If not backed up by a safety net, use all that you have to avoid hazards and mistakes. Do what it takes to be safe. Don't solo on slopes too steep for self-arrest. Keep three points of contact while moving the fourth. Focus; you know the drill.

The terrain mountaineers are willing to cross without a safety net is as varied as their personalities. If you begin to feel that a fall is possible and there are consequences greater that you can accept, do something about it. Add a safety system!

GLACIER TRAVEL TECHNIQUE

Consider a most basic rope system. Two people are walking along on a snow-covered glacier. Snow obscures the crevasses. If they make a route-finding error and accidentally step on a soft snow bridge, they will fall through it and tumble deep into a frigid place. Very high consequences.

You have already learned the skills necessary to catch your partner if she falls into a crevasse. Say you both tie into the rope and stretch it out so there is no slack between you. To make sure you both won't wind up on the same snow bridge, tie in at least 50 feet apart. With your ice ax in self-arrest position, you can now begin traveling up the glacier. You'll have to adjust the pace to keep slack out of the rope. In this scenario, if one climber falls in, the other will be able to catch her with a self-arrest in the snow.

In most low-angle glacier travel situations, this is the preferred belay technique: walking along, attached to your partner via the rope but not attached to anchors in any way. In the event of a fall, the partner can stop the falling climber with a self-arrest. She can accomplish this only because her rope system and the soft snow surface absorb most of the fall's energy. Make the system even more failsafe by climbing in a team of three so that two are available to stop a crevasse fall.

Remember, in every belay it is necessary to consider the four components of friction, position, anchor, and communication. Traveling on a snow-covered glacier usually offers a great deal of friction, though it varies with the snow surface. Softer snow offers excellent position; it is malleable, and the belayer can dig right into it when trying to stop the falling climber. Combining excellent position and friction with good technique that keeps slack out of the system so that a falling climber can't get going too fast and become difficult to stop eliminates the need for time-consuming snow anchors along the way.

If the slope is steeper, making position less effective, or if the surface is icier, creating less friction, you might need to consider adding anchors. By adding intermediate anchors, the rope is attached to the mountain, so that if the climbers fall, they are caught on the anchors and stopped. Anchors might simply consist of rope woven through rock protrusions on a ridge, but this would be very insecure. Better anchors might be slings tied around boulders or trees, or pitons or chocks placed in cracks in the rock.

Finally, consider communication. The climbers should pre-arrange some simple signals to help them keep their rope system as effective as possible. See chapter 8 for a more complete discussion of glacier travel techniques.

THE RUNNING BELAY

The running belay is a technique used on terrain in which the position of one climber would be insufficient to hold the fall of another. One of the most common mistakes in mountaineering is climbing together without protection in place on terrain so steep or difficult that one climber would not be able to hold the other's fall. The running belay is simply climbing together with intermediate anchors in place. It is usually employed on snow routes but is also useful in 3rd, 4th, and easy 5th Class rocky and mixed terrain.

In a running belay, the rope runs through running protection but the climber does not stop after one rope length to build a fixed anchor. Both climbers move along at the same rate of speed without allowing slack to develop between them. Each is the counter to the other in the event of a fall. Running pro, no fixed anchor—hence the name running belay.

Running belays can vary greatly in their level of security. A team of two might place only one piece between them if it is a

These climbers are moving together in a running belay. The leader places protection and the second retrieves it. If the leader falls, he will fall twice the distance from the last piece and then be stopped by the counterweight of his second. If the second falls, he will probably pull the leader off also, and both will tumble until the leader reaches the highest piece and is stopped. Place protection that will hold such falls.

very good one and if the terrain is low-angle enough that it will be easy to stop the fall. As the likelihood and consequences of a fall increase, the leader can place pieces more frequently to decrease the possible length of the fall if one should happen. Eventually the leader will run out of equipment. Before running out completely, some of it must be used to build a regular 5th Class anchor and belay.

Unlike the sometimes vague decision point between glacier travel technique and the running belay, which sneaks up on the unaware, the decision point here is more obvious. As the terrain becomes more difficult and dangerous, the team places more and more protection. Pretty soon, you'll be using gear so quickly that you'll be forced to place belays every rope length and you'll find that you're using a 5th Class system almost without having decided to do so.

FIXED LINES

A rope tied between anchors is a fixed line. Once in place, fixed lines allow several people to belay themselves across a section of difficulty or danger without having to use several ropes. When left in place over short distances that must be crossed many times or by many people, they add speed because the pitch does not need to be led again and the rope replaced each time. Large expedition-style climbs often leave fixed lines in place for several days while they ferry loads up to higher camps.

The friction for the self-belay on a fixed line should be supplied by friction hitches or mechanical ascenders. Ascenders are easy to manage but not as versatile as friction hitches tied with webbing or accessory cord. Ascenders can cut the rope in a severe fall, some models twist off in certain situations, and they hold in only one direction. Every wilderness mountaineer should have cordelettes or webbing that can easily be tied with either an improved prusik hitch or a klemheist onto a fixed line. Clipped to a locking biner on your harness, the cordelette or sling is a self-belay device. If you choose to free-climb with prusiks on a fixed line as a belay, consider using two in tandem to add security.

The climber's movement skills provide the position on a fixed line. Once the climber falls, he is out of position and fully loading the anchors. Since there is no belayer in position to absorb any of the load in the event of a fall, the top anchor must be fail-safe. There may be other anchors in the line holding the line in the correct place or anchoring the bottom. These, though important, are not nearly so crucial as the top anchor, from which the entire system hangs.

Communication is the final element necessary to consider. Since the climber belays himself, you might think that there is no need for signals, but the climber needs to know when it is safe to get on the line. Generally, because a fall by one climber would pull others off their feet, climbers travel on fixed lines one at a time. Because the lines are sometimes used nearby or in conjunction with 5th Class belays, the signals should sound very different from others. I have used the simple signal "The rope is fixed" instead of "On belay" to indicate to those below that the top of a line is "fixed," or tied into a good anchor.

THE 5TH CLASS BELAY

The 5th Class system, described at the beginning of this chapter, offers the most security.

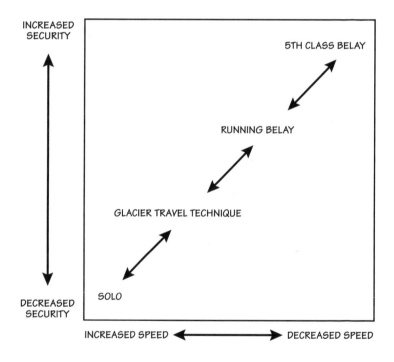

Safety systems that offer greater security often sacrifice speed. However, the potential time lost, pain suffered, and other consequences caused by using an inappropriate system for your abilities in the terrain are far worse than taking a bit of time to keep safe.

A LITTLE STORY ABOUT MOUNTAIN HAZARD

In 1985, two good friends and I ventured off to Mount Foraker to attempt an alpine ascent of the Talkeetna Ridge. It had not yet been climbed in alpine style—which means to climb from bottom to top in one push with everything you need on your back—so we were embarking on an ambitious journey. As is typical of many Alaskan expeditions, we flew in to our objective in a ski plane. Upon arrival, we set up base camp. We figured it would take a day to get to the ridge, five to climb it, and two to descend the Southeast Ridge and return to base camp. We added two days of food as a buffer and set off across the glacier under heavy loads.

We made a camp near the base of the Talkeetna Ridge, yet far enough away to be safe from avalanches that might tumble off that side of Mount Foraker. That night it snowed, depositing 6 or 8 inches in our camp, and who knows how much blew into various pockets higher on the peak. Ten miles from our base camp, we faced crucial decisions. We had nine days of food left, including two for storm days. We needed to keep that extra food in case of storms or problems higher on the peak and didn't want to waste a day's worth so early.

We discussed and debated the risks and options. The 1,000-foot gully we intended to climb to gain the ridge crest looked reasonable. It had no rock outcrops, the storm had not been a big one, and there was no sign of recent avalanches in the area. We were, however, all aware of the conventional avalanche wisdom: "Never climb within twenty-four hours of a storm."

But the storm had not been big. We thought that if a slide were to knock us off the mountain, there were no rocks to hit and the debris would run out to the flat glacier below, so we wouldn't be buried. Worried about our rations, and with clear skies above, we set off.

(continued)

MOUNTAIN HAZARD (continued)

We traveled across the glacier to the gully using the appropriate glacier travel technique: climbing together. We crossed the bergschrund, Tony in the lead and George second on the rope. I brought up the rear. The slope steepened: 30 degrees, 40 degrees, 50 degrees. It approached a steep 60 degrees at the top. Somewhere low in that steepening, we passed a decision point but made no decision. This was the crux of the climb, not in difficulty but in judgment.

Soon the slope became so steep that if one of us fell, the others would not be able to hold the fall. A misstep would send all of us tumbling down the long gully. As the angle increased only gradually, this hazardous situation crept up on us and we did nothing to protect ourselves against it. We could and should have done one of two things: attached ourselves to the mountain by placing protection and clipping it to the rope, or removed the rope and soloed. The first option, a belay, offered greater security. The arguments for the second option are that it is faster and that at least if one falls, it is only one—he doesn't drag the others down also. Instead, we climbed on, roped together but with no protection in place.

As Tony neared the ridge crest, the snow steepened to the degree that he pulled out his second ice tool for added security. As he plunged his ice tools into the snow, it cracked off to the right and left, and the entire upper snowfield moved as a unit down the mountain.

It began near the ridge, high, in a place where the gully had widened out into a small bowl. As we anticipated, the slab was not deep and was made of soft snow. It ran easily around Tony's feet and didn't knock him off. Seventy-five feet below, the gully was a bit narrower, so the snow piled deeper and moved faster, but George held on and he also stood through the avalanche's growing power.

(continued)

MOUNTAIN HAZARD (continued)

Still farther down the slope on the end of the rope, I stood in the narrow gully. George yelled, "Avalanche!" I looked up and there it came. That soft, 6-inch slab continued to deepen as the gully narrowed. Still I thought, "This will not knock me off!" I dug in my ax. I planted my feet, resolute in my conviction that I could withstand the force. In an instant I was hit and torn from the slope. The power amazed me. I felt a terrible pressure at my waist. George and Tony were holding me! My harness would surely cut me in half, I thought.

Suddenly, the pain at my waist went away, and we were hurtling down the slope. I had pulled my partners off.

The rope was like a slingshot. Tony caught me in an instant, his boots hit my face hard, and down we tumbled, tangled together. It was a long fall. At times I tumbled in the snow, at times I flew out into the air. Always I tried to get control of my ax and to stop myself. Several times I thought I had almost stopped, but Tony or George would pull me off and I would lose control of my ax again. I later learned that my ax had stabbed me seven times in the arms and hands while I was trying to grab it as I fell.

After what seemed like a very long time, during which I felt acutely aware of every little thing—my glasses came off and I had the time to reach out and grab them back—we slowed. We rolled; we stopped.

I could see Tony's face, eyes open with surprise and concern . . . and life. "George?!" we both yelled.

"I'm okay. Are you?" he responded.

Tony and I both replied that we were and laughed out loud, happy to have survived.

I replied that I was having a hard time breathing. Tony unbuckled a pack strap that had ridden up across my neck. We shook hands, Tony and I, congratulating each other for

(continued)

MOUNTAIN HAZARD (continued)

remaining alive. My glove spurted blood when he squeezed. There was blood everywhere, but we were too tangled in rope and snow to find all its sources. George came and helped us out of our ball of yarn. We were relieved to find that all the cuts looked to be the sorts we could fix ourselves.

Snow in all our clothes, we were cold and shaken and knew that we'd soon be hypothermic. We made our way to the flat glacier and spent the next hours drying, eating, and coaxing my cuts to stop their bleeding.

It was a harrowing day, nothing good about it at all. But in the days and years that followed, I was able to look back and learn a few things.

Why did we go up that slope in the first place? The schedule imposed by our rations, our unwillingness to compromise so early in the trip, a lack of knowledge about the avalanche hazard and rope systems, and the desire to get climbing on such a beautiful day and to succeed on the route all played a role.

Once the slope steepened to an angle that precluded arresting a partner's fall, we should have begun placing protection. That would have anchored us to the mountain and kept us from falling in the avalanche. At the very least, we could have taken the rope off. Then only I would have fallen (George and Tony were only pulled off by me). At least my partners could have been saved from the fall, which, at over 800 vertical feet, could have left us all unconscious with no one awake to perform first aid. Plus, I remember stopping only to be pulled off again. Unroped, it is likely that none of us would have fallen all the way to the bottom. Roped but without protection in place, we all went down.

Climbing together without running belays is certainly one of the most misused rope techniques in mountaineering. One should analyze situations continuously. If only I had

(continued)

MOUNTAIN HAZARD (continued)

asked, "What would happen if I fell right now?" I might have noticed that our choice of rope systems was inappropriate, and we could have avoided such a hideous event.

This also illustrates the many decisions and variables that play a role in accidents. All of the considerations that went into choosing to climb that day plus all of the decisions and indecisions that determined how we climbed had their role in that accident.

We were lucky and we learned something. But try telling a story like that to your mom!

CONCLUSIONS

It is important to see these various systems as a continuum of security and speed. Safety systems offer various levels of protection, depending on how they are created and used. They can be excessive, slowing and endangering parties unnecessarily. They can also be inadequate, failing to offer the protection needed when a fall occurs. These are all judgments that the mountaineering team must make. Questions of speed must be weighed against the need for security.

To keep the decisions simple, there is really only one question each individual must ask: "Am I safe right now?" Anchored, on belay with an adequate system, or comfortably soloing in appropriate terrain, the question remains the same. Once a team ensures that it is not taking unnecessary or unwanted risks, it is possible to consider other methods that might increase speed without unduly compromising safety.

6
Leading

Wilderness mountaineering demands that climbing teams be totally self-sufficient. Deep in the backcountry, far from roads and hospitals, all climbers must be capable of assuming a variety of roles, including everything from camp cook to doctor to route finder and navigator. Perhaps most important, on an isolated peak, all team members must be able to lead-climb. In the wilderness, you cannot count on a helicopter to pluck you from a cliff face or a local search-and-rescue team to lower you a rope. You must be able to take care of yourself, which means that anyone venturing onto steep, technical terrain in the wilderness should possess the knowledge and skill to lead to safety.

Your leading ability is an important safety skill to the entire group. Most alpine climbing teams are small, usually two to four climbers. If, due to unforeseen circumstances, teammates are incapacitated by injury or exhaustion, it is imperative that others be able to lead the team to safety if necessary.

Sharing the responsibilities of leading pitches also adds to a team's speed, efficiency, and readiness to make well-informed decisions. The classic partnership on steep terrain is a team of two, each climber leading a share of the pitches, or "swinging leads." This allows each climber to rest after the concentrated effort of leading while a ropemate leads the following pitch. Some pitches may be better suited to one climber's skills, so leads don't always alternate, but the most effective teams are made up of people with similar abilities and goals who are capable of sharing both the workload and the decision making.

Those who climb in the backcountry but do not lead are less likely to develop the acute awareness of hazard and route condition that is necessary to make informed mountaineering decisions. While leading, a climber must choose a safe, protectable line of ascent, place the protection, and thread the rope through it, all while concentrating on moving effectively and avoiding hazards. Leading demands total concentration and complete mental involvement in the climb.

Leading is a mental game of controlling fear, climbing well, and making myriad evaluations and decisions while engineering a complicated rope system. It is a skill that builds upon many others, including sound protection placement and knowledge of safety systems, an accurate and honest knowledge of one's abilities, and good, conservative judgment.

LEADING FREE CLIMBS

Free climbing is any climbing done without putting weight on artificially placed protection. The climber uses his hands and feet—along with "acceptable" aids like shoes, ice tools, and crampons—to ascend, with the rope system acting only as a backup. Once the climber weights the rope, a sling, or any piece of artificially placed equipment, he is aid climbing, even if the assistance is used only momentarily.

On a free climb, the leader invokes two safety systems: movement skills and the belay system, which serves as a backup. The components of movement as a safety system are an accurate knowledge of your abilities, ability to judge terrain and choose a safe route, and the skill to climb over that terrain without falling. If faced with the possibility of a fall, the leader must consider the options of down-climbing to the last rest or retreating.

The belay system is in place as a backup to catch the climber if the primary safety system fails. Depending on the climber, the difficulty of the terrain, and how that terrain accepts protection, the belay's effectiveness varies a great deal. On some pitches, the leader may be able to place gear so frequently that any fall would be quite short and unlikely to cause injury. On others, placements may be tenuous and widely spaced, making any fall extremely dangerous.

If the protection is good, steeper climbs can actually present less potential for injury because there is less to hit; on overhanging terrain, you may come gently to a stop in midair. More moderate, low-angle terrain that is fraught with ledges can readily injure a falling climber. When assessing a climb, the leader must recognize the consequences of a fall and be prepared to utilize the rope system in a way that minimizes risks.

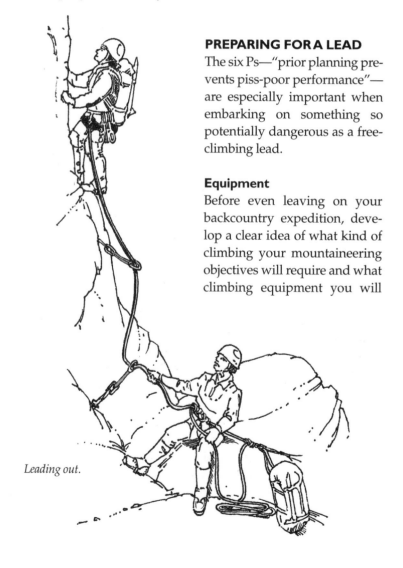

PREPARING FOR A LEAD

The six Ps—"prior planning prevents piss-poor performance"—are especially important when embarking on something so potentially dangerous as a free-climbing lead.

Equipment

Before even leaving on your backcountry expedition, develop a clear idea of what kind of climbing your mountaineering objectives will require and what climbing equipment you will

Leading out.

need. For almost any technical mountain route, two 45- or 50-meter ropes are mandatory. The ropes might be a single lead rope and another, smaller-diameter rope for rescue and rappelling, or double ropes that are used in tandem both on lead and for rappels. The single rope system is a bit easier to learn and manage, whereas double ropes are more versatile and lighter. No matter which system you choose, every mountaineering team should carry at least two ropes.

The protection that you take into the backcountry is more variable. Do you plan to climb ice routes? Rock routes? Snow? Or will the climbing be on a mixture of these mediums? If you fancy snow or ice routes, the equipment may still include some rock gear for anchors and protection placements on adjacent rock. Consider what might be needed on the routes in the area you're headed for or the specific climbs you have in mind. These pretrip decisions will limit your route choices once in the backcountry.

Once a specific route is chosen, build a rack that will meet the demands of that route. A rack is the selection of protection, carabiners, and slings that a leader carries up the climb. Anticipate the level of difficulty and the rope system or systems you will employ. Fifth Class systems require enough equipment for a belay anchor at the bottom of each pitch, the protection during the pitch, and another belay anchor at the top of the pitch.

Belay anchors aren't built as frequently for running belays, but a team benefits from carrying enough equipment to climb and protect long sections without having to stop, exchange gear, and swing leads. The size and type of protection needed will be determined by the nature of the route selected. Narrow cracks? You'll need small wedges and a selection of camming devices. Steep ice? Take ice screws and slings.

Most people carry a standard rack that is modified for the specific requirements of a given climb. A route with long pitches or hanging belays may demand more of everything. A thin crack demands more thin pro. Carry gear for each medium if the route is mixed.

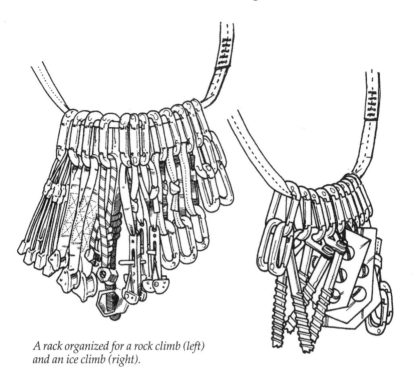

*A rack organized for a rock climb (left)
and an ice climb (right).*

The Belay Anchor

In most 5th Class lead-climbing situations, the belayer should be
anchored both against an upward pull in the event of falls held
through intermediate protection and against a downward pull in
case the leader is caught directly on the belay device. This means
including several pieces in your anchor to hold the large downward forces that could be generated by a fall below the belay. Frequently, less protection is needed for upward pulls, because they
are countered by the body weight of the belayer. You should also
build an anchor at the bottom of the first pitch so that leader falls
will not be lengthened if a belayer is pulled out of position and so
that you can tie off a fallen climber if necessary.

Before Leaving the Ground

Before beginning the climb, the leader should select and arrange
the rack so it will be as efficient and useful as possible. Rack the
gear on either a sling or gear loop worn over the shoulder or on

harness gear loops. Sometimes leaders use a combination of both methods. You will develop some personal preferences, but don't get too set on one arrangement. You may confront a pitch where gear usually kept in one place is more convenient in another.

The following are some helpful hints for racking gear:

- Put heavier gear toward the back of a sling or harness. Its weight will pull it toward your back and out from between you and the rock or ice.
- Rack gear in sequence from large to small so that you can go to the correct general vicinity of the piece you want without having to look.
- Especially with smaller pieces like stoppers, put three or four similar sizes on one biner. When you pull the biner off while on the lead, there will be several similarly sized pieces in hand to match with the crack. (Careful, you'll also lose three or four if you drop them!)
- Preplace biners on some of your runners and quick draws rather than having to build them at each placement.
- Larger pieces that are easier to size by eye can be racked one to a biner, as you'll be pulling them off accurately one at a time.
- Clip biners to your rack with the gates up and in. They'll be easy to unclip.
- Err on the conservative side—take plenty of gear. Difficult pitches use a surprising amount of slings, biners, and placements.

PROTECTING THE LEAD

Lead climbers thread their ropes through protection in an effort to have a system in place that will catch them if they fall. But there is a limit to how much gear you can carry and how much time you have. Within these constraints, leaders strive for as much safety as possible.

Place Protection Early

Placing protection early helps prevent ground falls and eliminate the potential for high fall factors. Perhaps the most dangerous portion of any pitch is the first few feet. Here, protection must be placed frequently enough to keep the climber from hitting the ground in the event of a fall.

Early protection is even more important when leaving belay ledges far off the ground. If the leader falls before the first piece is placed, he would fall below the belay ledge. The belayer must catch the climber directly on his belay device without having the rope go through a carabiner. The energy in such a fall—absorbed by only a small amount of rope—damages the rope and jeopardizes anchors.

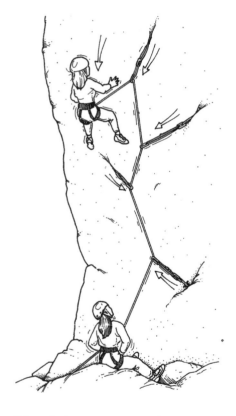

When placing your protection, keep in mind in what directions it will be pulled if you fall on it while it is the top piece, if it ends up as the bottom piece, or if it is somewhere in between.

The first pieces of a pitch serve another purpose. Much of the protection placed on the lead will hold a downward pull but is not set for an upward force. Falls generally pull down on pieces, so this seems reasonable. In reality, however, the protection placed during a pitch should be treated as a system rather than as a series of pieces that become obsolete when a new one is placed higher up. When a fall is held, the rope pulls up on the bottom piece and out on many of the others.

If the bottom piece is not set to hold multidirectional forces, the upward pull generated by a fall could pull the piece out. Upward force is then transferred to the piece above, which also may come out if it was intended to hold only downward pulls. This series of events can set off a chain reaction, causing protection to "zipper" out as successive pieces are tugged out by the rope. This is especially dangerous in the beginning of a lead, with only a few pieces between the leader and the ground. Leaders can prevent this possibility by making sure the first pieces are capable of holding an upward pull.

Place Protection Often

Place gear often enough to keep yourself from hitting the ground or a ledge in the event of a fall. The kinetic energy of falling climbers increases quickly as they gain speed. Thus, long falls mean more speed, more potential for hitting things, and much greater load on the rope system and protection placements. Leaders must take measures to reduce the length of falls.

Evaluate how long of a fall is acceptable. This decision has to do with the quality of each piece, the terrain in and over which the climber might fall, and what might be hit during that fall. Place protection with the knowledge that falls are unexpected events.

Place Protection Well

Much like the top anchor in a yo-yo top rope (see page 116), the piece of protection that holds the leader is a 2:1 pulley. The forces on a leader's top piece are more than the energy needed to stop the fall. Make sure protection placements are sound and will not be pulled out by the drag of the rope.

When placing protection on the lead, do what it takes to make each piece as effective as possible. This may include building an equitension anchor, because one piece alone will not hold, or using a locking girth hitch to keep a piece in place. It may mean placing protection often because placements look as if they will hold only short falls or body weight.

From as restful a stance as possible, look at the rock, ice, or snow near where you want the next placement. First look at the mountain, then determine what from your rack will best meet your needs. Let the terrain tell you what to place. A common mistake among novices is pulling a piece off the rack and then trying to make it fit the mountain. This does not work. Look and learn what the mountain wants, and then try to match a piece to the crack, depth of ice, or type of snow in front of you.

Once you have an idea what is called for, you can find the piece on your rack. Place it quickly. Add runners to reduce rope drag and direct the rope away from sharp edges.

Clipping the rope to the placement is often the most dangerous moment for the lead climber. If the rope must be clipped through a biner above your waist, you will be adding slack to the system while you pull it up to clip it in. This extra slack could lengthen a fall enough to make it far more dangerous. Be very stable and secure during the clip. Practice clipping a lead rope into carabiners with one hand before leading your first climb.

Once the gear is in, reevaluate the quality of the placement, check the route, and go.

Manage Your Rack

It may be important to conserve certain pieces or use them sparingly. Perhaps through visual inspection you know you might want to have a certain assortment of pieces later in the pitch or at the anchor. Don't overdo this, however. I have more than once saved a special piece I thought I'd need higher in a pitch only to "conserve" it for the entire climb.

As a general rule, I try to manage my rack so that at all times I still have a broad selection of size ranges left. If I'm getting low on small stoppers but have lots of larger pieces, I'll look for larger placements in order to conserve those small stoppers in case I need them later.

If you need a placement in order to keep the lead safe, conservation is a secondary consideration. You may be able to down-climb and back-clean that piece for use higher up or put in a belay before you reach the spot where it is needed again.

Place Protection Before Difficult-to-Protect Sections and Cruxes

In addition to solving the movement puzzle, leaders are faced with a certain protection puzzle. You may find it impossible to place gear during portions of many climbs. Wishing you had a piece nearby while in the middle of such a section will leave you feeling helpless. To avoid this, anticipate the difficulty of the movement and the availability of protection before you commit to a challenging section of a climb.

Place Protection from Good Stances

Choose good places to stop and place gear. It is both dangerous and physically and mentally taxing to place protection from tenuous or exposed places on the pitch. Try to relax on the holds from which you place protection. Investigate all the possibilities for making yourself more comfortable and secure during the procedure before you actually start work on the placement. On ice or snow, it is often advantageous to chop a nice foot placement or small ledge and place ice screws, pickets, or flukes from good rests.

Many leaders speak of situations in which, after placing a valuable piece of protection, they found a far more comfortable stance. Take the time to find those stances early rather than wasting energy and risking a fall during the placement process.

Consider the Followers

If a route travels straight up a mountain, the intermediate protection is valuable for the leader but is not usually necessary for those that follow. Once the second is on a top belay from a well-built belay anchor, the intermediate protection is not of much use. In a team of two, the second would remove all the gear while climbing the pitch. In a team of three, the second would remove all the gear except that which improves the belay for the third.

On a traversing pitch or section, the leader must take care to protect the climbers that follow. Anytime a pitch moves laterally, the leader must consider placements that would keep his second from swinging in the event of a fall. Often a leader will protect before a crux and then place little or no gear on the easy ground. On traverses, leaders must protect both before and after cruxes, and frequently enough to protect followers from long pendulum falls; otherwise, once the gear is removed by the second, the only intermediate anchors that could have prevented a long swing are gone, with the difficult move still to come! If there are more than two on the team, the second should clip the trailing rope to the piece and remove his top rope from it, leaving the gear in place for the climber or climbers that follow.

Don't forget to consider the problems followers may have with a pitch. Sometimes it is appropriate to leave a sling in place for a second to grab for a quick aid move. Sometimes a leader will place a piece specifically to show others the route or to keep the rope from knocking off rocks on others. Anticipating such problems for your second and offering the tools to solve them helps a mountaineering party head off long delays. Placing gear that is easy to remove also increases speed.

DOUBLE LEAD ROPES

Double ropes—generally two 8- or 9-millimeter ropes—are useful for many lead-climbing situations. Leading on two ropes allows you to clip one rope to protection that is off to one side of the climb and the other rope to protection that is on the other. This results in less zigzagging than would occur if one rope had to be threaded through such a system of gear.

Double ropes also allow the leader to make tenuous clips with one rope without adding slack to the other. In the event of a fall, he doesn't fall as far. And they are lighter than one thicker rope plus the requisite second every mountaineering team must carry. Double ropes are difficult to learn how to manage in a belay device, so if you do choose to climb on double lead ropes, practice.

LEARNING TO LEAD

Before even considering leading climbs, you must be competent and experienced with using the gear in the medium in which you plan to lead. Lead climbers generally spend a long apprenticeship as followers and top ropers before considering venturing out on the sharp end. Prerequisites for learning to lead include an accurate knowledge of your climbing skills, a proficiency with protection placement and anchor building, and a thorough understanding of all elements of the belay.

If you are ready to learn to lead, you can do mock leads and aid climbs to further prepare yourself. Practice for your first leads with mock leads protected by a top rope. Pretend you are on the lead, place gear, and thread a lead rope through that gear. Evaluate what might happen in a fall from each place on the lead. Have a partner climb the top rope to check and evaluate your placements.

Mock aid climbs are similar to mock leads, but here the climber stands on each piece with full body weight. Test the pieces vigorously by stepping into a sling clipped to each wedge or cam in different directions to see if it holds. (Be sure you'll be able to remove your placements!) Although body weight is no real test of the quality of a placement, the exercise does highlight weak pieces and the kinds of directions of force to expect during lead falls.

Be conservative on your first leads. Early leads should be on terrain that is well within your climbing ability Running and 5th Class belays on very easy ground help the novice get used to the systems and the feeling of having no top rope, with little likelihood of a fall. Your earliest lead climbs, due to lack of experience and unfamiliarity, can be the most dangerous. Take it slow.

LEADING AID CLIMBS

Another skill that sometimes serves the mountaineer well is aid climbing. Imagine yourself high on a route, many pitches off the ground, with one difficult pitch to go, when a cold rain begins. The crux looks dicey, especially in the rain. Your options include free-climbing the pitch with the increased likelihood of a leader fall, retreating via multiple rappels in hypothermia weather, or leading the pitch safely by doing a few moves of artificial aid.

For some, this kind of climbing offers its own rewards, and they seek big walls that demand many pitches of continuous aid. Big-wall aid climbing is beyond the scope of this text. What the wilderness mountaineer needs to know is the way to incorporate both isolated aid moves and whole pitches of aid efficiently into a largely free-climbing scheme.

Occasional aid moves are quite likely in wilderness mountaineering. Though you may peruse a guidebook before venturing into the backcountry, its information may be dated or inaccurate. Often, mountaineers seek out new routes or routes done infrequently and cannot predict whether the movement will be within their free-leading capabilities. Perhaps you'll approach climbing like *Accidents in North American Mountaineering* editor Jed Williamson, who says, "I don't use guidebooks, so every climb is a first ascent." And there is always the possibility that weather or conditions might change a route from an easy free climb to a tricky aid problem. Whether or not you choose to use guidebooks or research climbs in advance, be prepared for more difficult climbing than you expect.

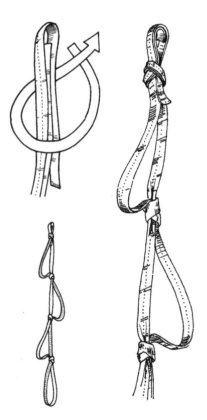

Climbing on artificial aid may be an equipment-intensive and tedious process, or it may mean using only one piece for a handhold in the midst of mostly free movement. Some climbs demand that the climber be "in slings" rather than on the rock for the entire route. If long sections of aid are anticipated, étriers—either pretied or sewn ladders made of webbing—should be taken along.

Traditional aid-climbing technique simply involves placing a piece of gear as high as possible and clipping a biner or runner to it so that the piece can serve a purpose as part of the belay. (So far this is no different

Tie four-step étriers out of 20 feet of flat webbing. Start by tying a Frost knot as shown and then tie overhands to make each step.

than free climbing.) Then the climber clips a sling or étrier into the piece with another biner and steps into it to test its strength. An étrier can be one loop or step, or it can be tied with several steps into more of a ladder. Once the leader feels it is secure, he stands up in the étrier.

A second étrier, on its own biner, clipped to the protection allows the leader to climb up the steps and gain enough elevation to place another piece and repeat the process. The higher each piece is placed, the faster the progress.

Étriers should always be clipped in with individual biners. They are much easier to unclip if other parts of the system, like the climbing rope or another sling, are kept separate.

Once a higher placement is made, checked, and weighted, the leader must reach back and retrieve the other étrier. Throughout this process, climbers make use of every available hold, whether it is natural rock

Leading an aid climb. The primary safety system is the aid climber's movement on his étriers and protection and any free-climbing holds he can find. The secondary safety system is a 5th Class belay threaded through the same protection.

or ice or an artificially placed piece. Aid moves are far easier with the creative use of free holds when available.

Aid climbing can be very strenuous. Often the climber must hold on to a biner or sling with one hand while fiddling with the next piece. In order to conserve strength, strive to find rests. One trick for obtaining a quick respite is to bend your knee. A quick, effective rest can be had by bending a knee to the outside of the étrier and sitting on your heel. If the belay rope is threaded through a high placement, tension from a belayer can take weight off your arms, as does clipping directly into a piece with a daisy chain made from a few biners.

While on aid, the safety system and the movement system rely on the same protection placements. Take care to ensure that the rope system is threaded through the most reliable pieces. It does no good to clip the rope high through a newly placed piece if it is an insecure one. There is no reason to add slack to the rope system by incorporating high placements that might pull out during a fall. Though the climber might be forced to move on aid placements that hold only body weight, these should not be included in the rope system. Once above such a weak placement, the leader can reach down and clean it for later use.

Aid climbing can be a basic tool that solves occasional mountaineering problems, or it can be a much more complicated and ambitious type of climbing that demands more skills than those discussed above.

Mountaineers need to be able to move quickly at times, and most make every effort to free-climb when possible. Occasional points of aid can be used quickly without étriers or other aid accoutrements. The ability to decide when to use a point of aid, place it, and move through it and back into free movement is an important skill for ambitious ascents.

7
Descending

Once you reach the summit,
Remember . . .
You're only halfway there!

The best descending system is walking down. If you've climbed a difficult route, walk off an easier way; this will be faster and safer. Sometimes, however, there is no walk-off. In these cases, you may need to rappel.

RAPPELLING

Rappelling means to slide down a rope. Although it is a common way to descend difficult terrain, rappelling should not be treated lightly. Ask experienced mountaineers, and they will say it is one of the most dangerous parts of the game. This is true for several reasons.

Rappels often happen at the end of the climb, late in the day. After the efforts of reaching a summit and the accompanying euphoria, the descent may seem a drudgery. The climber is tired, hungry, perhaps dehydrated; the day's excitement is past; weather and nightfall loom. Rappelling comes at a time ripe for error. Hanging directly from the rope leaves little room for mistakes in constructing the anchor.

Treat rappelling as any other safety system. Rappels involve the same four components—friction, position, anchor, and communication—the difference being that on rappel, you belay yourself.

Mountaineers use their bodies, a belay device, or a carabiner brakebar to supply the friction necessary to control speed. Body position during a rappel is important, and the integrity of the anchor is crucial as well. Clear communication helps members of the climbing party know what to do and when to do it.

Finally, the ability to retrieve the rope from the base of the rappel is vital. This is accomplished by passing the rappel rope through the anchor and rappelling on two lines. After the rappel, retrieve the rope or ropes by pulling on one end.

FRICTION

Almost any friction device can be used to control your speed on rappel. Many people carry special devices just for rappelling, but this seems like extra weight for an ounce-conscious backcountry traveler. Carry equipment that has more than one use to reduce your pack weight. Four options to supply friction for a rappel that do not require extra rappel-specific equipment are the body, the belay device, the carabiner brakebar, and the Münter hitch (a.k.a. the Italian hitch).

Body Rappels

A basic rappel can be created with only the rope, using the rappeller's body as the friction source. This technique can be painful and is not recommended for steep rappels where there is a great need for friction. The most popular body rappel is called a Dulfersitz. Like the hip belay, the Dulfersitz is not used often, but every mountaineer should master it in case of emergency. To make a Dulfersitz, face the anchor with the ropes, already thrown, between your legs. Pull the ropes up from behind and bring them around your hip, across the front of your body, and over a shoulder. Reach behind with the opposite hand and grab the ropes. This is your brake hand. If done correctly, the brake hand should be on the same side as the hip wrapped by the rope and the opposite side from the shoulder that is crossed by the rope.

Because friction will be concentrated where the rope turns around your body—the back of the leg and the neck or the top of the shoulder—pad these areas thoroughly with wool or cotton clothing. Nylon will melt under the heat of friction.

The Dulfersitz rappel emphasizing body position.

Lean back on the system without letting any rope slide through the brake hand, and then slowly lower yourself down the face by letting rope slip through your brake hand. There should be plenty of friction to control low-angle rappels.

Belay Device

Any belay device that will accept two ropes makes an excellent rappel device. Examples include the ATC, Clog Better-brake, and Pyramid. Many belay devices on the market today are built to handle a single rope very smoothly but are not capable of accepting two ropes. These devices, such as the Gri-gri and Wild Country's Single Rope Controller, are not useful for the retrievable rappels performed in the mountains.

Add a biner between a belay plate and your locking biner to make it more smooth if you are a small person.

Attach the ropes to your device as if the anchor were going to be the climber; your brake hand should be in or near the brake position for the specific device. You can make most devices slide more smoothly by clipping a biner onto the bight of rope between the device and your locking biner.

Carabiner Brakebar

If you don't have a belay device, a simple and very effective rappel system can be created with oval carabiners.

Six-carabiner brakebar system.

Start with either one locking biner or two standard oval biners, reversed and opposed, hooked directly into your harness. Clip two more carabiners, also reversed and opposed, onto the initial one or two. While facing the anchor, pass bights of both rappel ropes through these biners. While holding the bights, clip another carabiner under the bights and across the biners. When you let go of the bights of rope, they should lie down on the biners' spines. The spines serve as the brakebar.

You may find it difficult to get the last biner or biners clipped across the outer pair. To make it easier, clip the biner to one side of the pair and then push it across, gate down, and clip to the other side of the pair. Add another biner in the same position. Two biners should supply enough friction to control the descent of a lightweight person on a moderately angled rappel. If you weigh more, are wearing a pack, or are descending a vertical or overhanging slope, create more friction by adding more cross biners (brakebars). Most people prefer two biners, but three will fit.

Münter Hitch

The Münter hitch is best tied on a large locking biner, preferably a pear-shaped one. It uses little equipment but tends to wear and twist ropes.

Facing the anchor, tie a Münter hitch in each rappel rope, and clip them to your locking biner. The Münter hitch differs from a belay device in that the braking position is forward, toward the anchor, rather than back toward the hip.

Münter hitches on locking biner. Use a large, pear-shaped locking biner.

POSITION

The most comfortable and controlled way to rappel is to hold your body out from the rock by keeping both feet in front of you in an athletic stance. Keep your feet high and legs perpendicular to the terrain. If your feet are too low, they tend to slip, and your body may flop against the rock. Sit in the harness and control the rate of descent with your brake hand.

During a rappel, the fall line of the rope controls your path of descent. Follow the fall line. If you move out of that fall line, the rope will pull you back. This can happen suddenly, resulting in the rope sweeping across the face, bringing rock or ice down on you, or it may cause you to lose good body position and tumble.

When backing over the edge at the beginning of the rappel, make sure there is no slack in the system and that you weight the anchor in appropriate directions.

ANCHOR

Rappel anchors are an interesting problem because they are not retrieved; they stay in place. Therefore, questions of economic value and environmental impact are added to the anchor-building equation. No one wants to litter the wilderness with climbing gear, nor can most of us afford to leave a $100 anchor behind on each rap. Fortunately, safe rappel anchors need not be an environmental or a budgetary nightmare.

Rig your anchors with a minimum amount of gear; often a single piece of webbing—check that water knot—slung around a tree or boulder is adequate. If you question the integrity of an anchor, test it. Have the first rappeller fully load the anchor while it is backed up with other protection attached to the rappel ropes with a slight bit of slack. The last rappeller can remove the backup pieces before leaving.

Many times you will come to a belay anchor already in place. These fixed anchors should be fully evaluated and, if necessary, improved before you use them.

Above all, build an anchor that will not fail. All too many stories surface each year of people who, in their efforts to save a few dollars, build rappel anchors that fail, causing injury or death.

COMMUNICATION

Simple rappel signals keep a team from wasting time or making a mistake with the rope system. Here are some suggested signals:

Yell, "On rappel," to let your partners know you are embarking so that they can take cover from potential rockfall or offer a fireman's belay, a backup belay provided by a person at the bottom of a rappel by holding the ends of the rope. If the rappeller loses control or releases a brake hand, this person can pull the rappel ropes taut and stop the sliding rappeller.

"Rappel off," which has a different cadence from the above, lets others know that the rappeller is off the rope and it is free for others to use.

"All clear" indicates that the rappeller is clear of rockfall from subsequent rappellers. If a rappeller does not yell, "All clear," that means he was not able to find a sheltered spot, and others should take extra care not to dislodge rock or ice.

OTHER CONSIDERATIONS

Throwing the Ropes

Before you throw your ropes, make sure they are anchored. Throw the ropes one at a time in butterfly coils, middle first, then the ends (as described in chapter 4).

Dangers for the First Rappeller

The first rappeller may or may not know whether the ropes reach to an anchor spot below. You may be able to see that they arrive at a ledge or the ground, but it may be dark or the view may be obstructed. Therefore, the first rappeller should be prepared to build an anchor or to prusik back up the ropes if the route proves to be a bad one. Given this possibility, the first rappeller should take most of the rack and cordelettes along on the descent.

Many mountaineers put knots at the bottoms of the ropes to prevent the first rappeller from sliding off the ends. A figure eight tied in each rope works well as a safety knot. It's a good idea to use a friction knot such as a prusik as a backup. This comes off your harness and attaches to the rappel ropes either below or above the rappel device. (Once loaded, the friction knot is much easier to release if it's below.) If you're rendered unconscious by a falling rock, such a backup could save your life.

Whenever you are descending a steep cliff or you are unsure of the next anchor spot, a safety knot is a prudent precaution. Just be sure to untie them before you attempt to pull the ropes down!

Belays

A rappeller belays himself, but there are situations that might call for the addition of another belay to back up the rappeller's brake hand. A fireman's belay from below is helpful for all but the first climber. If you have only two ropes, consider having the first climber rappel on one rope, belayed by the other. The first climber can also be belayed by being lowered down the rappel route. The last climber usually gets a fireman's belay from partners already at the anchor or on the ground below.

Retrieving the Rope

Rappel on either half of a rope or two ropes tied together so that once the descent is complete, you can retrieve the rope by pulling one side. Use a Flemish bend to tie the rappel ropes together. This knot is easy to tie, untie, and inspect visually.

Take care when building the rappel anchor to minimize the friction of the ropes over sharp edges or irregular terrain; this friction might make them hard to pull. Choose a rappel route that is less likely to grab those ropes when you pull them. An extra few minutes to ensure that the ropes will pull smoothly through the anchor can save the much longer time it might take to lead or prusik back up to the anchor to free stuck ropes. Often you will need to lengthen an anchor or place it high in order to avoid acute angles formed by the rope bending over edges at the top of the rappel. Before leaving, the last rappeller should consider moving the Flemish bend over any edge it could get caught on.

Above all, check your route—try to find a descent that is clear of protruding rocks, trees, or shrubs that can grab your ropes when you pull them. Make sure you remember which rope to pull in order to retrieve the system, and finally, have the last rappeller remove any twists or tangles in the two ropes. A belay device facilitates this quite well.

Multipitch Rappels

Because the ropes are in use in the rappel system, climbers are no longer tied into their ends. Each climber should have a sling or cow's tail girth—hitched to his harness to use for clipping into each anchor. A cow's tail with a locking biner speeds and simplifies long descents.

During multipitch rappels, each person should always be clipped into an anchor, on belay, or on rappel. Be disciplined about clipping into the next system before unclipping from the last. Many accidents have occurred during brief moments when climbers have chosen to unclip at a rappel anchor.

Rappelling with a Pack or Heavy Load

Packs, especially if heavy, are tiresome on rappels. To make things easier, have a second cow's tail attached securely to them so they can be clipped to anchors quickly and easily. Wearing heavy packs can pull the rappeller backward. To avoid this precarious position, particularly on steep rappels, hang heavy loads down between your legs by a cow's tail hooked into the locking biner in your harness. This puts the load directly on the rappel system rather than on your body. Make sure you have enough friction to control your load.

If you are rappelling with a load that is difficult to lift, consider clipping it in at each anchor with a releasable hitch backed up by a slack cow's tail. When it is time to lower the load or rappel with it again, the releasable hitch (mariner's hitch, tied-off Münter hitch) allows for an easy exchange of weight from the anchor to another system.

Stopping in Midrappel

If you need to stop or free both hands during a rappel, there are several simple methods for tying off the rope. The easiest way is to wrap the rappel rope that is in your brake hand around one leg five or more times, then tie an overhand knot on a bight and clip it to your harness. This supplies enough friction to hold a rappeller in place while he builds an anchor, straightens the rope, or rests. Or, already have a friction hitch in place as a backup. Again, if it attaches to the rope below your rappel device, it is relatively easy to release.

LOWERING

Sometimes it makes sense to lower your partner to the ground. Maybe he's tired or hypothermic and doesn't feel capable of controlling his own descent. Maybe he's headed to an unknown anchor and wants to have the option of climbing back up with a belay if he can't find a good stopping place.

Lowering is accomplished by simply tying the climber into the rope and creating a regular 5th Class belay with a friction device. Recognize that the belayer must be anchored and positioned properly in order to hold the full weight of the climber for the duration of the lower. This procedure is similar to being lowered off a yo-yo top rope, but it is harder on the belayer because there is likely to be less friction in the system, especially at first. If your anchor is strong as it should be, consider attaching the friction device directly to the anchor to lower the climber. This will reduce the pain and strain on the belayer. Remember that it is usually wise to back up the lower with a friction knot attached to your harness.

When being lowered, the climber should lean back on the rope and assume the rappel position discussed above. If the climber does not give full control of the lower to the belayer, the system will be difficult to manage.

In some situations, lowering is faster. It is also a good way to get ropes down the route when wind is making it impossible to throw them. Similarly, lowering can provide a way to get heavy loads off a climb.

There are hazards involved in lowering both climbers and loads, however. Unlike rappelling, when a climber is lowered, he has no control over the speed of his descent. As a result, it is easy for him to lose his footing and slip against the face or knock rock or ice onto climbers below.

Lowered loads also tend to dislodge debris. One way to alleviate this is to have someone rappel alongside the pack to guide it. This reduces rockfall and helps keep the pack from getting stuck. Even with an attendant rappeller, it is usually too dangerous to lower packs when people are below.

SAFETY ON THE DESCENT

Even though climbers frequently choose less demanding routes and spend less time on descents, nearly half of all accidents reported in North America occur on the way back down. When preparing for any climb, consider it as a whole; plan for the approach, the climbing route, and the descent. Each is important and potentially dangerous. Have a plan for getting down, and leave time for it in your climbing day. Many climbers set a predetermined turnaround time to ensure that they will be able to get back down before nightfall.

Also realize that if delays or accidents occur, especially late in the day, when there is little time in which to maneuver, you may be forced to spend the night out. When you set out on any mountain route, be prepared to perform basic first aid, travel after dark, and survive a night if necessary.

At the end of the day, it is difficult to maintain the high level of concentration and awareness that the mountains demand. Be methodical and safe during mountain descents. On Latok III, a remote peak in northern Pakistan, my partner and I were forced to make twenty-nine rappels during a brief respite from a storm. We did not rush, however. We concentrated on each individual rappel—the anchors, ensuring that the ropes would pull, and belaying one another when appropriate. We did not think, "Let's hurry and get off this peak!"

After rappelling well into the night, with occasional short breaks to down water and food, we reached the flat glacier and made our way to a camp. By performing all the individual tasks efficiently and well—the ropes never stuck once and each anchor was safe—we descended quickly and, more important, safely.

8

Glacier Travel and Crevasse Rescue

All of the high mountain ranges in North America were carved into near their present form largely by glaciation during the Pleistocene epoch, which most of us know as the Ice Age. Some ranges are still deep in active glaciers, which continue to scour U-shaped valleys and create high alpine cirques. Mountaineers climb on many features produced by glaciation, including arêtes, horns, and polished walls. In addition, many of the approaches to these alpine playgrounds demand daunting travel over a glacier's snowy back.

Glaciers are rivers of ice fed by an annual accumulation of snow at their heads. The extraordinary pressure exerted by the buildup of snow and ice causes the ice below to become viscous and flow. Glaciers act like giant conveyor belts moving snow and ice down to their toes. This movement differentiates glaciers from stationary ice fields, which, because they don't have the requisite mass of ice, don't flow downvalley.

Near the surface, ice is not under pressure, so it remains brittle and tends to break and crack rather than flow as it moves around bends and over obstacles. Such cracks are called crevasses; they extend into the glacier as deeply as the brittle ice, which is about 200 to 250 feet. It is these cracks that worry the traveler; crevasses are hazards that differentiate glacier travel from any other form of travel. Snow covers and hides crevasses, turning them into traps awaiting the unwary and unroped. When the snow cover melts, cracks are easily seen and avoided.

Most prudent mountaineers use two systems to protect themselves from falling into hidden crevasses. First, they use a knowledge of glacial flow and crevasse formation to "read" the glacier and choose routes that avoid crevasses. Second, they rope together so that if one partner falls into a crevasse, the other can arrest the fall, and effect a rescue if necessary.

This chapter covers techniques for avoiding crevasse falls and for rescuing people from crevasses if falls occur. This is by no means a complete coverage of the topic. The objective here is to prepare the reader for basic glacier travel and crevasse rescue. If your plans include travel through difficult icefalls, or if glacier travel is a major component of your expedition goals, there are many fuller treatments of this topic available.

ROUTE FINDING

I have encountered many mountaineers who have such confidence in their route-finding skills that they sometimes do not rope up for snow-covered glacier travel. Faced with the prospects of a crevasse fall, they likely put extraordinary concentration into their route finding, but one miscalculation can have severe consequences. The mountaineer who route-finds as if unroped—as if his life depends upon it—and then also backs himself up with a rope system is traveling safely. Successful route finding depends on understanding the formation and predicting the locations of crevasses.

CREVASSES

Glaciers, which can be thought of as rivers of viscous ice, do not bulldoze hard rock out of their path. Instead, when downvalley flow forces ice against rock obstacles, pressure causes the ice to melt around the rock. The ice then refreezes on the downslope side when the pressure decreases. Once refrozen, the ice pulls or plucks material along as it moves. Rock that is massive and resistant to glacial plucking remains in place; the glacier flows around or over it. Hence a bulge in the underlying bedrock results in a bulge in the glacier—a convexity in its surface. This convexity creates tension in the brittle outer skin of the glacier—

tension that cracks the surface ice like the cracks in the brittle chocolate coating of a bent Snickers bar.

Crevasses form perpendicular to tension. So when a glacier's surface is convex for any reason, crevasses are likely. Tension can also be created when glaciers accelerate. Faster-moving ice on steep terrain pulls away from slower-moving ice on gentler slopes above.

Much of the tension in the ice is along the direction of the glacier's flow. The resulting cracks are called transverse crevasses because they lie across the path of the glacier.

Another source of tension is the stretch that occurs as ice moves faster around the outside of a turn in the valley. This tension often forms regular, radial crevasses that look like spokes on a wheel. On the inside of such meanders in the valley, compression in the ice and friction with the mountainside may cause a more irregular jumble of cracks.

Friction between the ice and the valley sides produces a drag on the glacier's borders along its entire length. The drag may cause marginal crevasses or may influence transverse crevasses by bending them into a herringbone pattern. The free-flowing central ice pulls away from the slower marginal ice and causes the herringbone patterns to point upstream.

Sometimes the interfaces between ice moving at different speeds causes small, oval crevasses and other odd cracks in the ice. Glacial ice moves with some of the characteristics of water, and crevasses sometimes seem to be the product of eddies, pools, and rapids of ice.

Very steep slopes, areas of excessive tension, or other activity in the ice often cause such extensive cracking that the crevasses interconnect in a jumble known as an icefall. In an icefall, crevasses dominate the landscape, and there may be very little surface left for travel. Mountaineers are sometimes forced to travel down in the crevasses rather than on the surface. Here the mountaineer faces greater difficulty from being unable to see ahead to find the route and greater hazard from active glacial ice hanging above.

Features in a glaciated mountain range.

When a glacier reaches its terminus, or toe, the ice tends to spread out as valleys widen and cease to compress the glacier from the sides. The resulting lateral tension may cause longitudinal crevasses. At the other end, the head of the glacier, giant transverse crevasses, or bergschrunds, form at the point where the flowing glacial ice pulls away from the stable rock, ice, and snow-fields above. This highest crevasse represents the point where the glacier begins to flow. Mountain walls above the bergschrund generally are steep enough to slough snow, never allowing it to deepen enough to gain the weight and the viscous character necessary to form a glacier. Frequently the stationary upper wall of a bergschrund is steep or overhanging and may be a significant obstacle on a mountain route.

Compression—in concavities, on the insides of bends, or at spots where the glacial flow is slowing—usually forces crevasses closed, so there are fewer crevasses and travel is safer. Excessive compression, however—like that which occurs when two giant rivers of ice flow together or during an extreme decrease in the rate of flow due to a change in the slope of the valley—can cause a mess of crevasses.

Route finding involves reading the tension zones and expecting the crevasses that may accompany them. The best single rule of thumb to use when choosing a route is that convexities in the surface represent tension and concavities indicate compression. Seek out routes that follow concavities. If troughs, valleys, or other low points are not obvious, level terrain will frequently offer fine routes. Avoid convexities—bulges, ridges, high points—in the glacier's surface whenever possible.

Sometimes crevasses may be visible through the snow. Prudence requires that the traveler consider any linear feature—a depression, a color change, even a shadow—to be a potential crevasse.

SNOW BRIDGES

The annual cycle of snow cover varies with a glacier's latitude and altitude. The upper reaches of Alaskan glaciers are never free of snow, whereas most glaciers in the Rockies and the Cascades melt down to near bare ice every year. Glacial zones that gain snow each year are called zones of accumulation. At the other end of the glacier is the zone of ablation, where there is a net loss of snow and ice each year. The firn zone, or firn line, is the transition point. Below it, the snow melts off and crevasses are easy to see and avoid. Above the firn line, snow remains deep and fills in or covers many crevasses. Near the firn line, the snow is melting and snow bridges over crevasses are more suspect and difficult to evaluate.

The firn line generally creeps up the glacier from spring through fall. Many subarctic and high-altitude glaciers continue to receive annual accumulations that hold the firn line low on the glacier.

When snow is deep, it covers crevasses and forms bridges across most narrower slots. Snow bridges offer routes across crevasses that would otherwise stop a team. But a weak bridge can be a trap, appearing strong and convenient but dropping away suddenly under the climber's feet.

Consider snowshoes or skis to make travel safer; they help disperse weight and can keep a climber from punching through a snow bridge.

MORAINES

Moraine is the rock debris moved downvalley and deposited by a glacier. Terminal moraines are left at the toes of glaciers and are most obvious when glaciers melt back, leaving the moraine as a free-standing hill. These huge piles of boulders and rocks, deposited within tens of thousands of years, form an unsorted jumble. The debris is often unstable and may make travel difficult. Very unstable moraines hide glacial ice deep below the rubble.

As glaciers pluck rock from the mountains at their sides, they develop another trail of debris along their margins. Known as lateral moraines, these rockpiles are often very active. Rocks plucked from below can undercut the slope above, resulting in rockfall and a growing pile of unstable debris.

When two glaciers come together, they drag their lateral moraines into the center of the new glacier. These moraines merge and create medial moraines along the interface between two streams of ice. Away from the rockfall at the sides of the glaciers and stabilized by surrounding ice, medial moraines offer reasonable travel paths in many instances. Though ice creeps into the moraine itself, rock tends to fill any crevasses, and substantial

medial moraines may be crevasse-free. NOLS expeditions traveling up the Matanuska Glacier in Alaska find that the easiest route
is on a 15-mile-long path of medial moraine we know affectionately as the "yellow-brick road."

While active moraines that are newly deposited and potentially unstable make travel difficult, older ones that have had
time to develop soil and plant growth sometimes offer excellent
routes. Travel along the sides of the Karakoram's huge Biafo
Glacier is easy where the lateral moraines have had time to stabilize but difficult where the glacier continues to scrape away at the
mountainsides.

PROBES

Predicting where snow-covered crevasses lie is difficult if you
rely on visual inspection alone. You can improve route finding by
using a probe to feel through the snow for solid ice or dense
snow below. An ice ax can be used to probe, but a basketless ski
pole or an avalanche probe is more effective.

Long probes are also useful for finding safe camping places
on a glacier. While on belay, one team member can probe the
snow deeply to determine whether an area is crevasse-free or is
covered by enough dense snow to prevent climbers from falling
through into hidden crevasses. A safe depth of dense snow varies
with climate and weather, but the probe should be at least 10 feet
long and the area checked thoroughly. To do this, the camp should
be checked every 2 or 3 feet in all directions and then marked
around the perimeter with bamboo wands 3 to 4 feet long.

Wands are also useful to mark routes. If you are traveling a
route that you plan to travel again, consider marking the route
every rope length with a wand. This is especially helpful when
trying to find the way back to camp during stormy weather in
featureless snow-covered terrain.

THE BELAY

On snow-covered glaciers, mountaineers rope together in order
to catch their teammates in the event of an unfortunate plunge
through a snow bridge into a hidden crevasse. In this situation,

Glacier travelers rigged and ready.

the falling climber is stopped by his teammates' self-arrest. The self-arrest combined with the rope acts as the belay system for glacier travel on low-angle terrain. As with any belay, to understand the system, it is best to analyze each of the components of friction, position, anchor, and communication.

FRICTION
The arrest of the falling climber is made possible by an immense amount of friction between the rope and the snow. Snow is abrasive, and as the rope comes taut between team members, it

absorbs a great deal of the energy generated by the fall. Rope stretch plus friction from the snow and friction created by the rope cutting into the lip of the crevasse all combine to reduce the force that comes onto the belayer. Harder snow surfaces offer less friction and reduce the effectiveness of the belay. On hard surfaces, as on solid ice, mountaineers do not rope up unless they have some form of protection beyond the self-arrest. Friction over the surface of the glacier must reduce the load coming onto the belayer or belayers enough that they can hold crevasse falls. If there is not enough friction, more than one person is likely to end up in the crevasse.

Fortunately, crevasses are more visible when the snow cover is hard or nonexistent. Climbers can see danger areas and add running protection or build an anchor and belay if necessary.

POSITION

Often so much energy is absorbed by the snow surface that the belayer hardly feels a fall at all. In more extreme situations—a longer fall, harder snow surface, or steeper terrain—the belayer must self-arrest in order to hold the fall. All members of the rope team must be prepared for a crevasse fall at any time. This means carrying the ice ax in self-arrest position and being ready to arrest at any time. Though a climber should yell, "Falling!" if he feels a fall is imminent, there may be no warning before the rope comes taut.

Keep slack out of the rope during travel so the fall of a climber is as short as possible. Not only does this make the fall less severe, it makes it easier for the belayer to hold. Light ropes, on the other hand, can make travel jerky, irritating, and confusing. Though slack must be avoided, this should not be taken to mean that tension is advised.

ANCHOR

Using standard glacier travel technique, a team does not place anchors or intermediate protection. Falls are held with a combination of only friction and position.

Anchors do play a role in glacier travel, however. Upon catching a partner with a self-arrest, one of the first things teammates on the surface do is build an anchor and transfer the weight of the fallen climber onto it. This is one of the first steps in the crevasse rescue process.

Glacier travel is a technique that has a finite realm of effectiveness. Other rope—systems 4th or 5th Class belays, fixed lines, and even rappels—may be more effective for some glacier travel situations, such as the following:

- Crossing fragile snow bridges when a crevasse fall is likely.
- Crossing snow bridges over wide crevasses where a fall might be long and difficult to arrest.
- Traveling over steep terrain where a self-arrest may not be effective.
- Traveling parallel with crevasses where the rope does not run perpendicular to crevasses and is therefore ineffective as a belay because it would slide along the lip rather than catch the fallen climber immediately.

COMMUNICATION

As with any belay, communication is essential to the smooth functioning of the team. Most communication is done through the rope and the actions of the rope team. It is the responsibility of followers, those not leading the rope team, to adopt the pace of the leader and keep slack out of the system. Tension or tugs from behind mean "Leader, slow down!"

Each member of a rope team must be ready for a crevasse fall and also help manage the rope. Most of the tasks involved in effective rope management do not need to be communicated verbally; plus, in most conditions, verbal communication along the length of the rope will be easily understood. But in situations where communication might be muddled by high winds, the team can reduce its communications to a few simple signals:

"Zero" means that the rope team should stop.
"Clear" means that the rope team should go.
"Falling" is a simple signal whose meaning is evident.

Travel while tied to others can be a frustrating endeavor. Effective communication and patience will help the team function well. If you find that your team is stopping or wasting time, or that communication is breaking down, take time to stop and discuss what changes and improvements are necessary to improve your efficiency; in the long run, these moments will save time as you travel up the glacier.

ROPING UP

How many people make a safe glacier travel team? Two is the minimum needed for a glacier travel belay. Imagine, however, one person holding a partner's long crevasse fall. Though this is possible, it is more secure for two people to catch a fall. It is also difficult for one person to perform the crevasse rescue techniques discussed below. Three people make a prudent minimum number for roped travel across a snow-covered glacier. This number allows for two people to counter a fall by the third. It also leaves a team of two available for any rescue maneuvers that might be called for. Four on a rope also works well. Five, though slow and difficult to manage, is the maximum.

The team needs to allow enough distance between members such that two will not be on a snow bridge at the same time. With three on a rope—one in the middle and one at each end—there will be 75 or 80 feet of rope between individuals, which is enough to span all but the biggest crevasses. Shorter distances, say 60 or 65 feet between climbers, are also adequate. Shortening the rope slightly between climbers can make travel a bit smoother, because there is less rope to manage. This also makes rescue somewhat more efficient, since the people at each end are carrying an extra 15 or 20 feet of rope, which may come in handy.

The people left on the surface must have enough rope to reach their fallen partner should they decide it is necessary to rappel to him. When the rope is divided evenly among members of a team of three or more and 15 to 20 feet are reserved at each end, enough rope is available between the two or more persons left on the surface. With a team of two, however, each member must carry sufficient additional length for rescue in his pack.

If someone on the team is less experienced than the others, that person should take the middle spot on the rope, and those members at the ends of the rope can alternate leading the team.

PREPARING A TEAM OF THREE FOR TRAVEL

Rarely in climbing do you clip into a rope with a locking biner; glacier travel is one exception, however. By using a locking biner, a fallen climber can free himself from the clip-in knot—and anything that might be hanging from it—to ascend the rope out of the crevasse. Usually, what is left hanging from the clip-in knot is at least a pack and perhaps a sled or skis. Climbing out of a crevasse is difficult enough without additional weight and encumbrance. Items left hanging in the crevasse can be hauled up later.

Standing on safe terrain—off glacier, off snow, or inside an area that has been checked and is crevasse-free—divide the rope in half, and tie a figure eight on a bight at the middle. Clip the knot to a locking biner on the middle person's seat harness. Those who tie in at each end should measure about 20 feet of rope from the ends and tie a figure eight on a bight. This knot is clipped to a locking carabiner on their seat harnesses. The extra rope ensures that when one of the team is hanging in a crevasse, those on the surface will have plenty of rope to reach him. It can also be used to clip in a pack or sled and prevents any shortage of rope during rescue procedures. The extra rope can be coiled over the shoulders or stashed in the top of the pack. If the end people choose not to shorten the rope and are carrying very light packs, it is preferable for them to tie the rope directly to their harnesses with figure eights on bights.

Climbers must check four points when clipping in for glacier travel:

1. The harness is on correctly and buckled properly.
2. The clip-in knot is tied and dressed correctly with adequate tail.
3. The locking biner is clipped properly through harness and knot and locked.
4. The teammates are attached to the rope correctly and ready for travel.

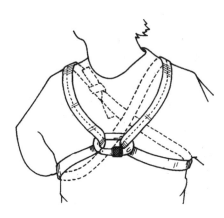

Improvise a chest harness with a sling.

If team members are carrying much weight on their backs, a sit harness alone may not be enough to hold a crevasse fall without injuring the climber. In this case, a chest harness—either presewn or improvised with a long runner—would help to hold a fallen climber upright in the crevasse. The rope (both ropes if you're the middle person) should be clipped through a locking biner on the chest harness.

Each climber carries a complement of rescue gear. At a minimum, this gear should include the following:

- One piece of protection appropriate for the snow surface (in addition to an ice ax).
- One short cordelette (or mechanical ascender), tied into a loop with a double fisherman's bend and used as a waist prusik.
- One long cordelette (or mechanical ascender), tied into a foot prusik as discussed below.
- One spare single runner.
- One locking biner to clip the rope to the sit harness.
- One locking biner to clip the rope through the chest harness (if carrying a heavy pack).
- One spare locking biner.
- Four spare oval biners.
- One lightweight rescue pulley.

The term *prusik* refers to a type of friction hitch and also to the ascending technique used with those hitches; as a result, it is used interchangeably with the word *cordelette*.

The cordelettes should be tied so they are ready to use for ascending, or prusiking, out of a crevasse. Before beginning to travel, the short waist prusik should be tied with an improved

The rope comes through the chest harness and is clipped with a figure eight on a bight to a locking biner at the harness. The end of the rope is clipped to the pack. The climber has his waist prusik on the rope and clipped to a separate locking biner on the harness, available to use as a belay device and ready if the climber should need it to climb the rope out of a crevasse. The foot prusik is stored on a gear sling or harness gear loop.

prusik hitch to the climbing rope and clipped to its own locking biner at the sit harness. Already on the rope, the waist prusik is ready for use and can serve as a simple belay device if needed.

The prusik hitch should be loose so that it does not bite into the rope and so that if someone falls in, loads come directly onto the clip-in knot rather than the prusik. The section of cordelette should be sized so that when a climber is hanging on it from a climbing rope, the hitch is just above head height.

The long foot prusik should be stored on gear loops on the harness. It should be tied so that a loop near its middle, created with a figure eight on a bight, can be attached to the climbing rope with an improved prusik hitch. One of the remaining ends can be girth-hitched over one foot, and the other end attached to a locking biner as the waist prusik. When standing on the foot prusik, the hitch on the rope should be waist-high on the climber.

CLIPPING IN THE PACK

If you are carrying a pack, the climbing rope is clipped through a locking biner on the chest harness. The pack should be clipped in also so that it can be removed and dropped in the event of a fall. For climbers in the middle, a short runner can be used as a cow's tail to attach the pack to the climber's clip-in knot. Use a separate biner. The end people can use either a cow's tail or figure eights on bights in the climbing rope about 4 feet beyond their own clip-in.

This leaves at least three spare biners, a rescue pulley, a single runner, and a piece of protection stored on the harness or over the shoulder.

RESCUE

Crevasse rescue, like any improvised rescue, requires the timely and creative application of a few simple techniques. Throughout the rescue process, it is essential that the surface team consider each step carefully. No procedure should be undertaken that could endanger the rescue team on the surface.

Self-rescue can be accomplished in one of two ways: either climb out of the crevasse with a belay from above or ascend out on your rope. If you choose to climb out, communicate your plans with your partners on the surface, and wait until they announce their readiness with "On belay."

If neither of these options is effective, the fallen climber must be rescued by his partners. To do so, the surface team must build an anchor, transfer the weight of the fallen climber onto that anchor, rappel to that climber if necessary to perform first aid, and raise him from the crevasse with one of various pulley systems.

BUILDING AN ANCHOR ON THE SURFACE

After a crevasse fall, teammates hold the fallen climber's weight purely by their position. Before anything else happens, that team must build an anchor to secure the belay. Communication may be impossible at this point, and the fallen climber could begin to ascend while the anchor is being built. Throughout the anchor-building process, be prepared to hold any subsequent pulls on the rope. Assuming that the fallen climber is one of the end persons, the following are the steps for making an anchor:

1. The middle person gets into a secure position and holds the full weight of the fallen climber.
2. The other end person proceeds toward the middle person on a self-belay by pulling slack through the waist prusik. He remains ready to self-arrest in case the middle person's hold on the fallen climber should begin to fail.
3. The end person continues past the middle person, still on a self-belay, toward the crevasse. About 10 feet past the middle person, he builds an anchor near the rope. Crevasse lips typically overhang, so the anchor should be built a safe distance from the edge (15 feet is a rule of thumb).
4. The anchor is attached to the rope with an improved prusik hitch in the end person's foot prusik. This is then attached to the anchor with a releasable hitch. A Münter hitch tied off with an overhand slip knot and overhand on a bight is effective (see chapter 9 for a complete discussion). Slide the prusik hitch forward until it is taut against the anchor.

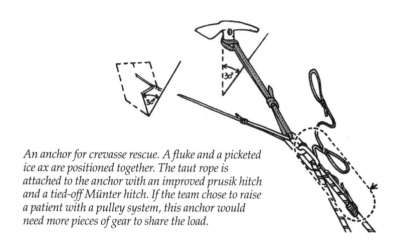

An anchor for crevasse rescue. A fluke and a picketed ice ax are positioned together. The taut rope is attached to the anchor with an improved prusik hitch and a tied-off Münter hitch. If the team chose to raise a patient with a pulley system, this anchor would need more pieces of gear to share the load.

5. The middle person now moves slowly toward the anchor, lowering the climber slightly onto the new anchor.

6. Before the middle person—whose position is still the backup for the newly built system—does anything else, the prusik attaching the fallen climber to the anchor should be backed up by tying the climbing rope directly to the anchor with an overhand slip knot and an overhand on a bight.

7. With the fallen climber anchored securely, the rescue team can send one person to the lip of the crevasse. This should be done quickly, since the fallen climber may be in dire

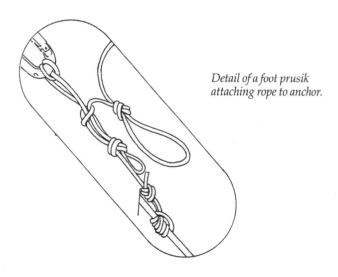

Detail of a foot prusik attaching rope to anchor.

need of aid. Generally it is easiest for the free end person to go to the edge with a belay from the middle person or a self-belay from his waist prusik.

ASCENDING OUT OF A CREVASSE

The plunge into a crevasse is often sudden and unexpected. If you have fallen into a crevasse, it is imperative that you stay calm and think clearly. "Alaskan slow bake" may characterize conditions on the glacier's surface, where the sun and snow create a giant reflector oven, but temperatures deep in a crevasse are usually quite cold. It is crucial to work quickly in order to avoid hypothermia.

A heavy pack poses an immediate challenge for a fallen climber. The weight can pull you backward, making any task difficult. First remove the pack. It is attached to the rope independently of you, so it won't be lost. Quickly don clothing to ward off hypothermia and keep your fingers dexterous.

On the surface, your partners will be building an anchor as rapidly as possible. As soon as that's done, you can expect one of them to come to the crevasse lip to check on you. If it looks like the best option is to climb or walk out of the crevasse, don't begin until you can communicate with your partners so that as you make your way, they can put you on belay. Sometimes a climber can be safely lowered a few feet to terrain that offers a route out.

Unfortunately, the walls of most of the crevasses that catch glacier travelers are difficult to climb. Often the snow or ice is steep and topped with an overhanging lip of softer snow. Therefore, getting back to the surface usually involves some method of ascending the rope. Since ascending does not increase the load on the line, you can begin ascending immediately if you are able to even though your partners may still be working on an anchor. You will need your waist prusik, which should be on the rope, and your foot prusik.

First attach the central loop of your foot prusik to the rope with an improved prusik hitch. Clip the loop on the foot prusik's short end to a locking biner on your harness. Tie the longer end to your foot with a Clark's hitch.

Ascending the climbing rope out of a crevasse. The foot prusik is attached to the foot by a girth hitch. Make this more comfortable by sliding one part of the girth hitch behind the heel (Clark's hitch).

You may have to unclip your chest harness from the rope to move the hitches freely on the rope. Push the waist prusik up high and tight. Bend your knee and move the foot prusik up to within an inch of the waist prusik.

When you straighten your knee and stand up, hold yourself close to the rope, as you move your waist prusik up. Then sit down in your harness again. This is your rest position. If your pack is below you, its weight will inhibit any upward progress unless you unclip from the rope. Make sure you weight your prusiks before you unclip to ensure that they are working correctly. In your rest position, you will be held by the waist prusik and backed up by the section of your foot prusik attached to your harness. If you are not carrying a pack, it is safer to remain clipped or tied to the rope.

Ascending out of the crevasse is now a matter of standing on your foot prusik and moving up your waist prusik, then sitting in the harness and raising your foot while you move that prusik up. Practice this hanging from a tree or a crag at home before you ever venture onto a glacier; familiarity with the motion and equipment will make the entire process easier in a real situation. You will find that fine adjustment of your prusiks allows more elevation gain with each move.

In a crevasse, the soft snow near the lip tends to create the biggest problems. The force of your fall will have caused the climbing rope to dig deeply into that snow, and as a result, you won't be able to finish ascending on the original rope. But by the time you reach the point where the rope vanishes into the snow, one of your partners will have had the time to belay himself to the edge with a bit of extra rope. He can drop a length of that rope into the crevasse for you to ascend. In order to keep it from digging into the soft snow, the rope should be run across an ice ax shaft or over a pack (anchored, of course, so it won't fall into the crevasse). To finish your ascent, you must transfer to this newly placed rope.

In order to do so safely, tie a figure eight on a bight in the new line, and clip it to your harness with a locking carabiner. Then, while anchored from the new line, transfer your prusik system to it and finish ascending out. Your partner will still need to help you over the lip.

IF THE FALLEN CLIMBER CANNOT SELF-RESCUE
Frequently a fallen climber will need help getting out of the crevasse. This help may range from giving the person a hand over the lip to hauling that person out of the crevasse with a pulley system. If the fallen climber is injured or unconscious and cannot climb or ascend out of the crevasse, the rescue must be performed by the surface team. In some situations, first aid for the fallen climber is a priority, and a team may decide that one member must rappel to the fallen climber immediately. Sending a rescuer into a cold crevasse is a serious decision and should not be made lightly, particularly if it leaves only one person on the surface. As always, safety of the rescuers should be considered paramount.

A rescuer who rappels into a crevasse should be sure to take anything necessary to improve the rope system, begin first aid, stay warm, and get himself back out. Rappelling in to a victim is a committing and time-consuming process. Many rescues can be achieved without having to send a rescuer into the crevasse.

When a rescuer goes to the crevasse lip, he should take enough equipment to prepare the crevasse edge for hauling the climber out. Ropes under tension cut deeply into the lip. This is one of the greatest hindrances to crevasse rescue. The rope on which the climber is hanging will likely be hidden in the snow, and the hauling system should be built with a new rope over a prepared lip. The lip should be padded as explained in the previous section.

Hauling a fallen climber out of a crevasse involves producing enough lifting power to raise the weight of a person through the friction created by the snow. At NOLS we frequently have the luxury of having many people available to help with such a rescue; in these cases, it is often quick and simple for many people to grab the rope and pull the fallen climber out of a crevasse. Smaller teams, however, must create some mechanical advantage in order to raise a helpless person.

Raising Systems
Rope teams of three or four usually need to create a pulley system in order to gain the mechanical advantage necessary to raise their partners. Like a yo-yo top-rope anchor, which "feels" twice the force of a falling climber, the fallen climber in a pulley system will feel twice the force for each pull on the rope.

In a 2:1 pulley system, the rope slides through a pulley attached to the load. The rope moves twice as far as the load does, so the energy needed to move the fallen climber is spread out over twice as much distance. You actually do the same amount of work, using half the energy for twice the distance. A 2:1 system is also called a C pulley, because the rope makes sort of a C shape.

In most crevasse rescue scenarios, however, the surface team needs even more mechanical advantage and must produce a 3:1 system, or Z pulley. In a Z pulley system, a pull on the rope is multiplied into three times that pull on the fallen climber. You may have used a 3:1 system without knowing it. Many people use a simple Z pulley in the form of a trucker's hitch to tighten tent guy lines.

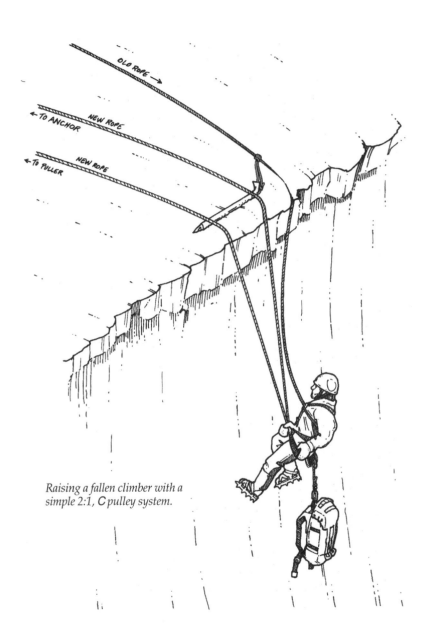

OLD ROPE →

← TO ANCHOR   NEW ROPE

← TO PULLER   NEW ROPE

Raising a fallen climber with a
simple 2:1, C pulley system.

To create a Z pulley and raise a fallen climber from the crevasse is relatively simple. You can use either the original climbing rope or a new end dropped to the fallen climber to set up the system. Before beginning anything, however, the middle person should clip directly to the newly built anchor with a cow's tail and untie from the rope. After that, the end person can begin setting up a Z pulley. The following steps are for a system made with the original climbing rope:

1. Self-belay with a waist prusik to the edge of the crevasse and check on the fallen climber.
2. Ascertaining that the appropriate course of action is to haul that climber out, pad the climbing rope to prevent it from digging deeper into the snow.
3. With a cordelette, tie an improved prusik hitch on the fallen climber's rope as near to the edge of the crevasse as possible.
4. Clip the rope near the end person to the cordelette with a carabiner.
5. Return to the anchor with the rope that has been clipped to the cordelette. This is the rope you will pull with. It is a belay rope, and hands on it are brake hands.
6. Undo the overhand backups that tie the climbing rope to the anchor. This leaves the climbing rope clipped through a biner on the anchor.
7. Now a tug on the rope that comes from the cordelette at the lip will raise the climber. One rescuer should monitor the prusik hitch that originally held the fallen climber to the anchor and keep it from sliding into the pulley system. Leave it on the rope, however, as a "ratchet" that can be used to hold the climber if the lip cordelette needs to be moved back toward the lip to allow for further raising.

If a climber is deep in a crevasse, the cordelette that began near the lip will reach the anchor before the fallen climber gets to the surface. In this situation, you need to reset the system. Tighten the ratchet prusik, and then lower the weight of the climber onto it so that the anchor is holding the load. Then one rescuer can loosen the other prusik and slide it back to the edge, and the raising can resume.

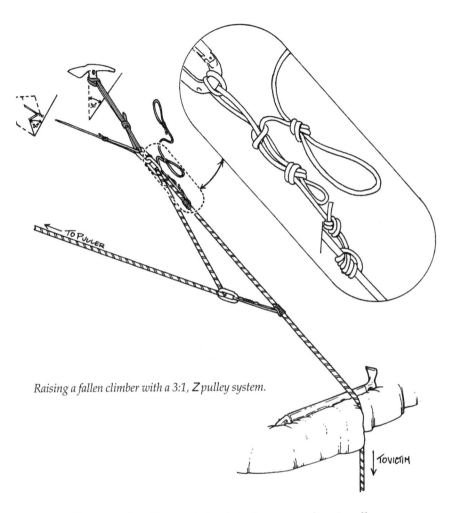

Raising a fallen climber with a 3:1, Z pulley system.

Beware of pulling a victim into the snowy lip. A pulley system allows the surface team to generate a huge amount of force, and if the victim is pulled up against a snowy lip, injury is possible. If you mistakenly pull a victim up against the lip and the ratchet prusik grabs and holds him against the snow, you can release the slip knots and slack that ratchet prusik to lower him a bit.

In reality, these pulley systems lose a great deal of their efficiency to the friction lost as the rope bends acutely around pulleys. Mountaineers further increase that loss to friction by using carabiners at the pulley points rather than carrying the extra weight of a true pulley. Using carabiners as the pulleys, a 3:1 system results in a mechanical advantage of only about 2:1.

Sometimes a 3:1 system is not enough, and the rescue team must create even more mechanical advantage. This is just a matter of piggybacking pulley systems. The figure below shows how to piggyback a 2:1 on a 3:1.

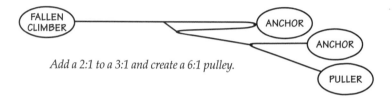

Add a 2:1 to a 3:1 and create a 6:1 pulley.

IF THE MIDDLE PERSON FALLS IN

Trying to rescue a fallen middle person can be awkward. One end person must hold the weight of the fallen climber while the other builds an anchor as near to the lip of the crevasse as seems prudent. The fallen climber can then be held on the anchor while the team member who orginally held the fallen climber maneuvers around the crevasse to help with the rescue. If this is not possible, once the fallen climber has been lowered slightly onto an anchor, the rescuer who has been holding the climber can then move a bit nearer the lip and build an anchor of his own. One rescuer can then perform a raise on one anchor while the other backs up the process by belaying and pulling with the other rope.

ONCE A VICTIM IS BACK ON THE SURFACE

Throughout any form of rescue process, the team should be sure to maintain basic glacier travel precautions. The climbers should not gather together unless they are sure they are on safe ground and a fall is not possible.

Once a crevasse fall victim is back on the surface, first aid becomes a priority. In addition to traumatic injuries, the victim may need to be treated for shock or hypothermia and may need rest before traveling again.

Before the team starts to travel again, members will have to belay one another until the rope is stretched out and they are back into their positions on the rope.

CONCLUSIONS

Glacier travel techniques vary greatly among mountaineers. Each climber seems to develop a favorite way of ascending a rope and getting out of a crevasse. Each seems to find a unique progression of steps in crevasse rescue. The techniques presented in this chapter are simple ones that work with a minimum of extra equipment.

Many carry mechanical devices—ascenders—for use in ascending out of crevasses and creating pulley systems. They are not worth the extra weight unless you plan an expedition that entails many miles of difficult glacier travel. Many climbers carry extra ropes to facilitate difficult crevasse rescues, while at the other end of the spectrum, some travel unprepared and lack both adequate skill and equipment.

You need adequate gear and practiced skill so that you can improvise rescues in any situation. Glacier travel is a necessity on the approaches to many of the world's big mountains. It can be safe and quite spectacular and enjoyable once you begin to understand route finding and become comfortable with the rope systems.

9

Improvised Rescue

Rescues are diverse and unpredictable. They may involve injuries, perhaps major ones, or they may merely involve getting yourself or someone else out of a difficult position. You may need to handle something as simple as figuring out how to rescue yourself when, having fallen off an overhang, you dangle in the air, unable to reach the rock. Or you may need to reach a partner who is unconscious, two-thirds of the way up a lead. These situations typically happen at inopportune moments, and if not dealt with effectively and efficiently, they can escalate into much larger problems.

Prudence may be a virtue and an ounce of prevention worth a pound of cure, but what if the climb doesn't go as planned? There are certain skills that are useful to have when faced with unforeseen problems high off the ground. You should not consider these skills to be rote procedures for solving predictable problems; rather, think of them as techniques that, once understood and practiced, can be used in a variety of combinations to solve a myriad of problems, from mundane to life-threatening. Before getting too remote from help and advice, before embarking on a multipitch climb onto a snow-covered glacier, practice these tricks to help you prepare for the problems that may await you.

In wilderness mountaineering situations, there is no one to rely on but yourselves, so you must be able to improvise a rescue and perform first aid. In this chapter, worst-case scenarios are used to illustrate rescue techniques. Consider, for example, the possibility of a fallen climber who is unconscious despite wearing a helmet. In this situation, you must be able to reach the climber, perform first aid, move him up or down to the ground or nearest ledge, and then maintain him until you can get medical help. This example involves complicated techniques, but if you master the skills required to enact a successful rescue in this situation, you will have no trouble handling more routine problems.

In belayed terrain, solving mountaineering problems usually involves advanced rope work. Solutions are based on a package of skills and concepts that can be adapted to many situations; practice is crucial to their usefulness. Though these techniques accomplish rescues and save lives, they are also useful for more common maneuvers, such as freeing the hands during the belay process to put on a jacket, or retrieving gear from low on a pitch to reuse it higher up.

Rope skills are only some of the tools necessary to solve problems in steep terrain. Judgment, creativity, and an ability to evaluate the situation and choose the correct course of action are all equally important. Paul Petzoldt used to say that when faced with an emergency, it was best to take a moment and smoke a cigarette—in other words, take a few moments to think and plan before going into action. If you are well acquainted with rescue systems, able to choose the appropriate technique, and practiced enough to perform it quickly and efficiently, you will make up for any time spent planning your course of action. Remember, use the simplest methods available. Fortunately, careful mountaineers rarely need to invoke rescue techniques. Unfortunately, as a result, the skills tend not to receive the practice they deserve. It is important to take the time to review them, and also teach your partners—they may need to rescue you!

Whether you plan to lead, follow, or just tag along, the skills explained in this chapter are essential and will benefit anyone who plans to travel into 4th or 5th Class terrain, especially if it is remote. A complete understanding of the belay in all its variations is a prerequisite to the skills discussed here, and knowledge of first aid is essential. Additionally, you need to be competent enough at tying knots that you can tie them one-handed, behind your back, in an icy rope that is rattling in the wind, at night, in a hailstorm, and with your mittens on.

ASCENDING AND DESCENDING FIXED LINES

Mountaineers frequently encounter problems that can be solved with simple answers. In rescue situations, getting yourself out of trouble is often the simplest solution. To rescue yourself, you have a variety of options: climb to safety, ascend or descend the climbing rope, or build an anchor and clip into it. The most common example of self-rescue is ascending a fixed line out of a crevasse after falling through a snow bridge (see chapter 8).

Fixed-line ascension is not just used for rescue. On very long and difficult walls, teams often haul gear in a bag rather than carry packs. It is faster to anchor the rope at the end of your lead and have the second ascend the rope on prusiks—or, more easily, on mechanical ascenders—than to have him climb the pitch. This leaves the leader free to haul a bag up while the second cleans the pitch. Climbers also ascend taut lines to reach fallen lead climbers and sometimes descend fixed lines to help an injured second.

TYING OFF A BELAY ROPE

In order to do much more than simply "slip, slap, and slide," a belayer must be able to free both hands yet still secure the climber with the rope. This involves tying a knot, or adding friction behind the friction device, to replace the brake hand. You can also tie off a belay rope to anchor a climber at a belay ledge while he prepares to lead the next pitch. Tying off the belay rope is usually the first step in any improvised rescue, and the method you use should be reversible under a load. In a 4th Class belay or when using glacier travel techniques, your hands are already free, so this technique is not relevant.

The simplest way to tie off a climber, or yourself while on rappel, is to wrap the rope around one leg until there is enough friction to hold the brake line (five to seven wraps). To be safer, you can tie an overhand on a bight behind the leg wraps and clip it to your harness or to the guide rope.

If you are using a sticht plate, another technique is to tie it off with two half hitches on bights (be very careful not to let your fingers get caught in the knot). Clip the bight to the guide rope as an extra precaution against the knot slipping.

If you are belaying with a Münter hitch, you can tie it off with a slippery overhand and an overhand on a bight. Clip the bight to the guide rope.

Each of these maneuvers accomplishes the same thing: It ties the climber to the belayer's waist and frees both hands for other tasks. The climber is still on a belay, albeit a nonadjustable one. All of these options have an important advantage: The hitches, overhands, or leg wraps can be released even while the rope is loaded.

Use two half hitches after passing the brake rope through the locking biner to tie off a belay. A mule knot and an overhand on a bight are also acceptable.

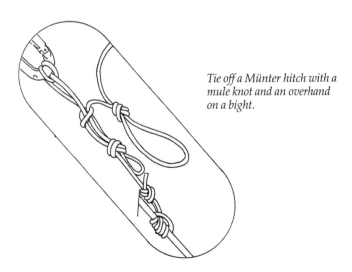

Tie off a Münter hitch with a mule knot and an overhand on a bight.

ESCAPING A BELAY

If the climber is conscious and first aid is not a pressing concern, you may choose to remain in the system and set up a simple rescue, perhaps a quick 3:1 pulley to help him through those last few feet to the belay. If first aid is imperative, or your presence in the system inhibits rescue, you must escape the system so that you can go to the climber or for help.

Once you leave the system, it will no longer have the advantage of belayer position, so your first task is to evaluate the anchor and determine whether it is adequate to hold the fallen climber. The belayer rarely has access to gear that is not already in the anchor, so it is important that the possibility of a belay escape be planned into every belay, especially if it is off the ground or if the pitch looks to be a long one.

Improve the anchor if necessary. If you were climbing together (as in glacier travel), you must build an anchor. If you are unable to make an anchor sound enough to hold the patient without the inclusion of belayer position, you cannot escape the belay.

When both hands are free and the anchor is adequate, tie an overhand on a bight in a long cordelette to create a 6-inch loop. With the loop, tie an improved prusik hitch or klemheist on the climber's rope. Then tie the other end of the cordelette directly to the anchor with a Münter hitch and a mule knot. Slide the klemheist or prusik until there is no slack between it and the anchor. If you cannot reach the anchor with the cordelette, extend it with available rope from the stack.

Now you can release the tied-off belay (leg wraps, half hitches, or mule knot) and slowly lower the load onto the cordelette. There should be enough slack for the belayer to leave the belay. Before doing so, however, you must be comfortable with the safety of the system holding your patient. The crucial links in the system as it stands are not backed up, and they can fail at very low forces, so before you leave the system, back it up! (A prusik hitch tied with 6-millimeter perlon on 11-millimeter perlon fails at 1,200 pounds.)

Tie the climbing rope directly to the anchor with a Münter hitch tied off with a mule knot. The reason for a Münter hitch

Belayer with a climber tied off and prusik anchoring climbing rope.

rather than another knot is that if the prusik or klemheist fails and the load comes onto the backup, the Münter hitch can be released, whereas a knot could not. If you will be lowering the patient and are escaping the system so you can get help or more rope, the Münter hitch is ready for use in the lowering process.

Reduce the potential for an unnecessary shock load if the friction hitch fails by working slack through the backup knot at the anchor before removing the climber's rope from your friction device.

Now you are free to untie from the anchor and maneuver. Remember, protect the rescuer! Make sure that whatever course of action you choose now is safe. You should be working calmly and methodically; if you find yourself nervously fumbling with knots, stop and take a few very deep breaths to regain calmness so that you can consistently do things right the first time.

REACHING A FALLEN LEADER

When a leader falls, he is left hanging from a single intermediate anchor point high off the ground; a fallen second hangs below a belay anchor. In order to do any first aid, you must go to the patient. If the patient is below you and you have enough extra rope, rappel. Be sure to take prusiks or slings so that you can reascend the rope if need be. If the patient is above you and there is not enough rope left in the stack to lower him to the ground or ledge, you may have to ascend his rope using cordelettes.

If you have a spare rope, you can belay yourself as you ascend. Stack the rope neatly on the ground and tie one end to the anchor. Ten feet away, tie a figure eight on a bight and clip it to a locking biner on your harness. As you ascend the climber's rope, clip the other into reliable intermediate protection. You can improve intermediate placements as you go if necessary. When you reach the end of your first 10 feet, measure 5 more, tie a figure eight on a bight, and clip that to your harness. Unclip and untie the original figure eight. After 5 more feet, repeat the process. Using this method, you can belay yourself. Depending on the situation, you may choose to clip in more or less frequently. For example, as you climb farther from the ground, you might choose to clip in less frequently, since a longer fall is possible before you hit anything.

If you don't have the luxury of enough rope to reach the fallen climber, you will have to prusik up or down at least some of the line without the benefit of a separate safety line. This is a scary undertaking.

If you are ascending to the patient, your weight will not add to the load on the top piece. The weight of the fallen climber is matched by an equal holding force in the anchor; therefore, the force on the top piece of protection is equal to twice that of the climber alone (minus the force absorbed by friction in the system).

When you weight the rope, you will replace the anchor as the counter to the fallen climber's weight. The load on the top piece is roughly the same in either case, unless you are rough when ascending the rope. Excess activity can add downward tugs and hence add force to the top piece of protection—the piece on which both of your lives depend. Ascend using the best approximation of the system discussed in chapter 8 that you can manage with the equipment available. You will do your patient no good at all if you ascend in an unsafe manner that risks both of your lives. This is a dangerous undertaking.

After reaching the patient and performing first aid, you can use the lead rack to beef up or build an anchor, clip the patient into that anchor with a cow's tail, and free the rope so you can either rappel with your patient or lower him to the ground or the nearest large ledge.

REACHING A HELPLESS SECOND

In most cases, a second can simply be lowered to the last belay ledge or the ground. But sometimes lowering an injured or unconscious second will put him in a bad spot.

Ascending a rope.

If you are descending a weighted line to the patient, your weight will increase the load on the anchor. Fortunately, you are starting from the anchor and can evaluate it carefully before deciding to descend the rope.

Consider rappelling using the rope in the stack. One option is to free one end of the rope and throw it down as a rappel line. Make sure the rope is anchored and that you take cordelettes along in order to reascend the rope later. It is possible to rappel off of extra rope without leaving a knot at the anchor. In this case, the weight of the fallen climber acts as a counter to your own. This technique allows the res-cuer to retrieve the lead rope once he has reached and anchored the victim, but it is a difficult balancing act and should be practiced thoroughly before being attempted in the field.

LOWERING

The simplest rescue is to just lower the patient directly to the ground. After performing first aid, return to the anchor, release the overhand backups, and lower the climber with a Münter hitch directly on the anchor. If you need to lower the patient more than one rope length, tie on a second rope and pass the knot through the lowering system. If you must lower a patient more than the total length of rope available, you may find it faster and simpler to rappel with the patient.

RAPPELLING WITH A PATIENT

This is yet another technique that is virtually impossible to perform alone with an unconscious patient.

Placing the patient on your back is an option, but this is very difficult for the rescuer. An easier method, if the patient is conscious, is to place your friction device and locking biner at the end of a short cow's tail (the friction device should be no more than 3 feet from your harness). Hang your patient from the same friction device on a slightly shorter cow's tail. With this method, you can control both your descent and that of your patient with your brake hand but do not have the burden of a person on your back.

If you are going to a small stance or to a hanging belay rather than the ground, you will need help from the patient or another person to anchor the patient. An autoblock hitch tied on the rappel rope near the brake hand and attached to the rescuer's leg loop offers a helpful belay for the team. The autoblock does not need to be monitored and is easy to release by lifting the leg it is tied to.

CLIPPING PATIENTS INTO ANCHORS

When you clip a helpless patient into an anchor, use a releasable hitch such as a mariner's hitch or a Münter hitch and mule knot. Either should be backed up by a slack cow's tail. This eases the process of unclipping the heavy person from the anchor. When you are ready to rappel or lower again, put the patient into the rappel or lowering system, unclip the slack cow's tail, and then release the mariner's hitch. As in any climbing situation, having the person rest on a ledge—good position—with the anchor as a backup system helps keep the odds against accidents more in your favor.

The mariner's hitch.

PASSING KNOTS WITH THE END OF THE SECOND ROPE

The ability to pass knots through lowering systems allows you to use longer sections of rope and increase the speed of an improvised rescue. If you have attached two ropes together for a long lower, you will have to pass the knot (a Flemish bend is recommended) through or around the friction device. This is much easier with two people, but it can be done alone. You will need one cordelette, a second rope, and a second friction device or locking carabiner in addition to the lowering system already in place to pass a knot without compromising the patient's belay.

When you have only 5 or 6 feet left in your first rope, tie off the climber with half hitches or a mule knot/overhand on a bight combination. Stack out the second rope, and tie the top of the stack to the end of the climber's rope with a Flemish bend. Attach your cordelette to the climber's rope near the friction device with an improved prusik hitch. Tie a figure eight on a bight in the standing end of your second rope, and clip it to the cordelette. Place that rope in your second friction device (which should be clipped directly to the anchor), and take in slack until the cordelette is taut. Tie off the second friction device with a releasable tie-off. Rather than let the entire system rest on a prusik hitch, back it up with a figure eight on a bight tied in the second rope about 5 or 6 feet from the Flemish bend, and clip it to your anchor.

Now untie the tie-off on your primary system, and lower the patient until the secondary system is loaded. Either work the Flemish bend through the friction system or take the rope out, move the knot, and replace the rope in the friction device. Pull the knot back as close to the friction device as possible, and tie the system off again. Untie the figure-eight backup, untie (with brake hand in place) the second system tie-off, and lower until the primary system again takes the load. Make sure you retrieve your cordelette before lowering further, or it will move out of reach and cause all sorts of problems. Now you may untie the primary system's tie-offs and continue to lower.

PASSING KNOTS WITH A CORDELETTE ALONE

This method is recommended when the load is easy to hold and to manage. It is exactly the same as the technique discussed above, except that the cordelette serves as both the friction hitch and the secondary lowering line. You need only your long cordelette and a locking carabiner in addition to the lowering system.

Stop lowering when the Flemish bend is about 18 inches from the friction device. If it gets any closer, you risk forcing the knot up against the device, a problem that can be remedied only by raising the patient back up a few feet—no easy task. With leg wraps or half hitches, tie the climber off. Now, with both hands free, tie an overhand on a bight in one end of your cordelette, making a loop about 1 foot in diameter. Attach this loop to the line going to the climber with a prusik hitch. With the remaining tail of the cordelette, tie a Münter hitch on a locking carabiner clipped into the anchor. Slide the prusik right up against your friction device, and take slack up through the cordelette Münter. Tie off the cordelette Münter hitch with a slippery overhand and an overhand on a bight. Rather than let the entire system rest on the cordelette for even a few moments, tie a quick figure eight on a bight 2 feet behind the Flemish bend on the second rope, and clip it to the anchor.

Now set the prusik, and lower your patient the few inches necessary for the cordelette to take the load. You should now have enough slack at the friction device to allow you to either work the knot through it or take the rope out and replace the friction device with the knot just below it. Make sure the Flemish bend is placed snugly against the friction device before going on.

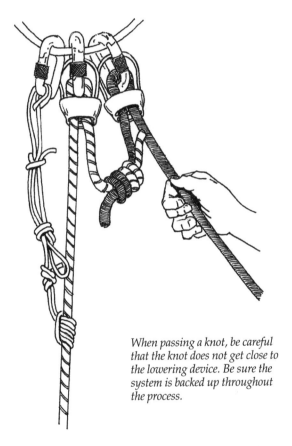

When passing a knot, be careful that the knot does not get close to the lowering device. Be sure the system is backed up throughout the process.

Place your brake hand back on the lowering line or, better, tie it off with half hitches. Release the overhand backups, and gently lower the patient until the original friction device again takes the full load. Before you begin lowering again, remove your cordelette or it will be carried off as you lower.

As you can imagine, this demands a great deal of practice before you're called upon to perform the technique with a real patient. Minor miscalculations in the amount of cordelette needed to accomplish the knot pass will mean possibly dropping the patient a few inches or even feet and unduly shock loading that suspect top piece.

RAISING

Raising is very difficult. If you've practiced raises and are faced with the decision to raise a climber, you will know whether it is possible. If you haven't practiced, the rescue situation is not the time to learn how to raise! Even the most elaborate pulley systems offer little real mechanical advantage, and it is virtually impossible to raise an unconscious patient alone. The most common application of raising systems is crevasse rescue. These techniques, outlined in chapter 8, can also be used on rock or ice if necessary.

A belay device allows a belayer to create a quick 3:1 pulley to help a tired or injured second finish a pitch. With a short loop of cordelette, tie a prusik hitch on the rope, and clip a biner to it. Clip the brake rope through the biner with your guide hand. When you pull with your guide hand, it replaces your brake hand, which can then slowly relax. Replace your brake hand and hold the climber in place when you need to reset the system.

Raising completely unconscious patients is more challenging. The 2:1 and 3:1 pulley systems discussed in chapter 8 can put large loads on anchors and ropes. If you choose to initiate a raise, make sure the rope does not run over sharp edges, and beware of injuring a patient by pulling him up against an obstacle such as a small overhang.

CONCLUSIONS

Lone rescuers with unconscious patients can perform very few of the procedures discussed. Because rescue situations so commonly arise, parties of two on glaciers are not advised. Small teams are at a distinct disadvantage in any rescue situation, and a two-person mountaineering team must avoid such situations with conservative, thoughtful climbing. Imagine the difficulty involved simply in transferring an unconscious patient from an anchor to a lowering system by yourself. If you want to see for yourself how difficult it is, try it with a partner acting as the unconscious patient.

When you travel into the wilderness, you automatically take certain risks. Rescue and first aid for true medical emergencies is unlikely at best. In well-trained parties of three or more (NOLS courses avoid travel in parties of less than four), the likelihood of effectively solving problems is good. With only two, circumstances can quickly become very dire unless the patient's injuries are minor.

If you spend much time pursuing wilderness mountaineering, you must assume that something will one day go awry. With this in mind, it makes sense to prepare for that day by learning and practicing a bag of tricks. These skills, along with the judgment and creativity to use them well, may one day save your life or that of your partner. More important, practicing these skills may help you foresee potential problems and avoid them altogether.

After becoming familiar with these rescue problem-solving techniques, you may find that as you look up at a climb or sit happily on belay ledges, your mind is filled with "what ifs" and endless worst-case scenarios. Though this sounds as if it might ruin an experience altogether, that is not the case. These mental gymnastics only serve to keep you out of trouble and boost confidence. You will find that confidence in your team's ability to solve all but the rarest and worst problems only makes your mountaineering experience more enjoyable.

10

Style and Ethics

Each clown may rise
And climb the skies,
When he hath found a stair.
But joy to him
That dares to climb
And hath no help but air.
—*George Wither*

Early mountaineering was a game without rules. When the Incas climbed to the tops of the Andes, the Shoshone reached Wind River summits, or Wymper summitted on Mont Blanc, mountains had the upper hand. Helicopters and oxygen bottles did not exist. We now have the technology to reach any summit on earth by "unfair" means. So climbers have developed a set of self-imposed rules, or style considerations, to keep their game challenging.

The merit of a mountain climb, as it is viewed by other climbers, depends on the route and its relation to the means used by the climber. The most difficult and beautiful mountain, climbed with the aid of a helicopter, holds little value as a mountaineering achievement. If the climber employs more limited means or, to use mountaineering vernacular, better style, the ascent becomes a greater achievement.

The mountaineering goals you choose, the manner in which you attempt them, and the way you define success make up the style of your climbs and expeditions. Mountaineering style is an individual's personality reflected in the mountain environment. The result is an infinite variation of climbing styles and dreams that range along an extraordinary spectrum. Some value the challenge of free-climbing the most difficult lines; some seek to test their nerve. Many mountaineers enjoy beautiful places or value the camaraderie with teammates, while others place a premium on the speed of their ascents. A number of those who climb in remote backcountry enjoy climbing routes that, as far as they know, have never been done before.

Mountaineers often strive to climb as purely as possible, using a mimimum of technological advantage. Using less aid and assistance makes an ascent more unlikely and difficult and hence is seen as a greater accomplishment. Placing value on the style of an ascent is the mountaineering community's way of maintaining the idea that there are climbs left in the world that are impossible.

Beware of letting another's idea of high style cause you to embark on objectives that, because you adopt someone else's notions of purity, are too difficult, dangerous, or simply not enjoyable. Climbing styles are like personalities; each person's is unique. Do not worry over the way your own style rates or ranks. Each of us approaches climbing for different reasons and rewards, and with our own ever-changing definitions of "success." Most questions of style have no real effect on any but the climbing team, and many mountaineers are unconcerned about the accomplishments of others. Your relationship with the environment, your partners, and yourself is what matters. Pressure to perform and competition among climbers often result in overextended climbers making poor decisions. And only you know how successful you may be on a climb.

> *You get up or you don't. And even if you got up you are quite aware of how you got up. There is no fooling yourself, no matter how it looked from the ground. You know if you had insufficient control of your mind, if you panicked or were on the edge of panic, if you clambered up, emotions in turmoil,*

gripped, despite outward appearances of calm and cool. . . .
Even the minimum climb often requires so much of a person.
Even a slight exposure to climbing seems to cause beneficial
changes which from other disciplines might result only after
years of concentrated effort.

—*Rick Sylvester,* A Clandestine Plea

It matters little how you climb until you begin to affect the experiences of others. When an ascent begins to affect other climbers or the environment, it becomes a larger, ethical issue. A team that litters the mountains and harms the rock changes the experience for those that follow. Every team should be self-reliant and capable of either avoiding accidents or solving problems without adversely affecting others or permanently scarring the mountain.

SELF-RELIANCE AND CAUTION

It is selfish for a team of climbers, by virtue of their own ideas of style, to extend themselves in such a way that they endanger the lives of others who must come to their aid. Anytime a rescue is called for by a mountaineering party, the rescuers—helicopter pilots, searchers, first-aiders—risk their own safety when they venture out into the mountain environment. Self-reliance, to the extent that a team does not frivolously call for rescue or plan trips in which the likelihood of such a call is high, is imperative to keep the "game" of mountaineering from endangering or bringing tragedy to others. If you agree that it is unfair to endanger others or inflict tragedy on friends and family, then self-reliance and caution in the high peaks are imperative.

When a climber's concern for how others perceive his or her accomplishments begins to play a role in that climber's route choice and decision making, peer pressure has influenced style in such a way as to impinge on or affect that climber's judgment. The styles of other climbers need not play a role in your climbing experience.

ENVIRONMENTAL ETHICS

The success of your expedition can be rated by its footprint on the landscape. The environment is an unwitting participant in the game of mountaineering. Once the wilderness was a huge expanse and a dominant force on this continent. As Americans fought it back, more always seemed to remain. Now it has dwindled to only 4 percent of the U.S. land base, and we are faced with the possibility of its vanishing completely.

All mountaineers and backcountry travelers should observe "leave no trace" principles, enjoying the wilderness without harming it. Guided by a few simple principles, the mountaineer can easily move through the landscape without changing it. In order for wilderness mountaineering to be possible in the future, we must not destroy the wilderness or the mountains. Strive to place as much value on the environmental ethics of your expedition as you do on your mountaineering achievements.

THE PRINCIPLES OF "LEAVE NO TRACE"

1. **Plan ahead and prepare.** Plan your expedition with an eye to minimizing your impact on the land and its inhabitants. Reduce the amount of potential litter you take into the backcountry by leaving extra food packaging at home. Know what kinds of camping practices you will have to use in order to leave no trace, and be prepared for them. For example, wood is scarce near treeline, so take a stove if you're planning an expedition to such an area. Know who administers or manages the land, and recognize rules, laws, and considerations.

2. **Travel and camp on durable surfaces.** Use existing impacted areas such as trails and campsites in order to allow pristine areas to remain less touched. This includes keeping vehicles on legal roads and hiking on trails, never beside them.

   No group should venture into pristine areas at all unless members have the skill and inclination to leave no trace. If you do so, travel in small groups, spread out tents, and move camp frequently so that your effects on the area will not add up. Camp on ground that is either free of vegetation—rock, sand, or snow surfaces—or covered with durable vegetation like grasses. Avoid beauty spots that others will likely choose and may develop into high-use areas. Camp at least 200 feet from water. Try to eliminate any sign of your passage when you break camp.

Avoid transitional areas where overuse is just beginning. Refrain from camping or walking on terrain that has been used a bit but that still shows signs that it could easily recover its pristine nature. Areas recently trodden or camped upon are at the greatest risk of being pushed over the threshold into highly impacted areas.

3. **Dispose of waste properly.** This means everything: trash, food waste, toilet paper, and all forms of camping and climbing equipment. There are mountaineering situations that, because of safety considerations, cause a team to leave the occasional rappel anchor or fixed protection placement. These are serious environmental decisions that should not be taken lightly. Please pack out anything you can.

Human waste can be absorbed safely into the natural environment in one of two ways. (Be aware, however, that in well-traveled public lands, such as some national parks, regulations prohibit these techniques and require that waste be packed out.) Waste can be buried in a 4- to 6-inch deep "cathole" dug in organic soil. The active ecosystem of dark, organic soil decomposes the feces. Catholes should be in inconspicuous places, at least 200 feet from water, and should be well covered and disguised. If all you have is scree or sand, burial is still the best option.

On large glaciers where no organic soil is available, dig a deep latrine or use a narrow crevasse. The pathogens do not decompose but are diluted in the immense volume of snow, ice, and water contained in the glacier.

Wash dishes with hot water, no soap. The waste water can be scattered over a wide area away from camps and water sources. If you are in bear country, wash water should be concentrated in a sump hole to reduce its odor. Soapy water must not be allowed to enter streams and lakes. Wash and rinse water should be kept at least 200 feet from water sources.

4. **Leave what you find.** Leave campsites as you find them by choosing sites that don't need any "improvement." As NOLS instructor Rich Brame, the philosophical force behind "leave no trace," says, "A good campsite is found and not made." If you move a rock to make your sleeping site more comfortable, put it back. Avoid damaging plants, including those on climbing routes.

   Leave natural and cultural artifacts for others to see and enjoy. Land managers consider the preservation of cultural artifacts a high priority. Federal law prohibits the removal or disturbance of archaeological resources.

   Leave the rock as you find it; it is a limited resource that never recovers from impact. The definition of wilderness is "untrammeled by man," and frivolous scarring of rock is unacceptable.

5. **Minimize the impact of fires.** Because wood is generally scarce high in the mountains, mountaineers must almost always use a stove.

   Sometimes wilderness travelers enjoy the warmth and feeling given by a small campfire. If you choose to cook on fires or build them occasionally for fun, make sure the area you are camped in has enough firewood to support your fire. Gather only wood that has fallen to the ground and is smaller than your wrist. Larger limbs and trunks contribute nutrients and habitats to the ecosystem and are difficult to burn completely to ash and to disguise totally. Breaking wood off trees leaves visible scars. If there is not enough wood on the ground, there is not enough wood in the ecosystem to support a fire.

   If there is a preexisting fire ring, use it. If there are several in one high-use area, consider consolidating them into a few or one. Destroying fire rings in high-use areas is largely futile, however, for they will be rebuilt.

In pristine areas, look for an exposed area of mineral soil on which to build your fire. You can find mineral soil in dry riverbeds and on sandbars. Sand won't catch on fire as organic soil can. When you are finished, be sure to burn all wood completely down to ash, which can be scattered once cold. Remnants of a fire in a riverbed wash away with the next rain.

It is possible to move mineral soil and build a mound of it to protect plants or rock from the heat of a fire. Mound fires allow fire building anywhere. Carry the soil in a stuff sack, and pile it into a large mound 6 to 8 inches thick. When you are done, dismantle and disguise the mound. Scatter the ashes and replace the soil.

6. **Respect wildlife**. Be especially considerate of nesting falcons and other birds in alpine routes.

7. **Be considerate of other visitors**. As options for true remoteness continue to dwindle, backcountry users must take care not to destroy the solitude and wildness other users seek. Backcountry etiquette helps many users enjoy an area without getting in the way of one another's experiences. Taking breaks well off a trail, camping away from others, keeping noise pollution to a minimum, and avoiding routes that others are already climbing are some simple methods that can enhance the wilderness experience for others. In many parts of the world today, spires, peaks, and pinnacles that capture mountaineers' imagination may be sacred to local people, and on such sacred peaks, climbing may be prohibited. The Navajo nation, for example, denies access to Shiprock and Spider Rock for such reasons. In India, expeditions to Nanda Devi and Shivling are prohibited.

Take the time to research local custom for any area you visit. It may mean abiding by the societal customs in a foreign land or a different part of North America. It may also mean abiding by the climbing ethics of a given part of the world.

Concern for local peoples not only prevents conflict but can also provide the opportunity for you to benefit from the friendships and support that might result.

These minimum-impact principles merely describe the basic methods for leaving no trace. Preserving the wilderness depends on the awareness and willingness of each visitor to make such practices a priority. Overuse of popular areas, litter, contaminated water, unnecessary bolts, and rappel anchors all contribute to civilization's increasing encroachment on the small areas of wilderness left. The "leave no trace" principles represent minimum standards of practice for any user.

Nonetheless, these techniques only minimize human impact; they do not eliminate it. And a few people abusing pristine lands can undo all the efforts of a majority of minimum-impact users. If you hope that there will be wilderness left in years to come, you must put these principles to work every single time you enter the backcountry. And if you agree that fire scars, litter, and damage to the rock are impacts worth avoiding, realize that there are many larger threats to pristine lands. Minimum-impact camping practices are a way to visit the wilderness without creating excessive impact. But if you truly want to see it thrive, you might consider more active efforts at preserving wilderness.

WILDERNESS BEGINS WITH YOU

No matter where you find your wilderness experience, at some point you may discover the need to fight for that land. This can become a lifelong commitment. Many people say, "I don't have the time" or "I don't know what to do to make a difference," but the truth is that each individual does make a difference, and there are simple and productive ways to do so. The following are a few ideas:

1. Understand land management and stewardship. When land management agencies begin making plans, there are public-comment periods during which you can submit comments related to your experiences and personal knowledge of an area. Your intimate understanding of backcountry conditions can be invaluable to managers. This may be as simple as identifying camping areas that see too much use or areas that, because you love them, should be preserved.

2. Get involved with conservation organizations. You may find that conservation groups can also use your expertise. If you feel that a local or national group works toward goals you agree with, join it.

3. Make your views known to Congress. In the United States, funding for land management and protection comes through appropriations from Congress. Writing letters expressing your views about recreation and wilderness management is essential for the future health of public lands. Despite what you may believe, political leaders respond directly to the opinions of people like you.

4. Register when you travel on public lands, and ask permission if the land is private. Registration is a small effort that can help record the actual activity on public lands. Funding for public lands is often directly justified by the number of users. Trail maintenance, campsite cleanup, and backcountry patrols can preserve the pristine qualities of wilderness. These activities will not occur if funding is not available.

CONCLUSIONS

The future of the mountain wilderness depends on how you, its users, care for it. But in order to be effective, minimum-impact practices must be matched by similar efforts when you are not in the backcountry. What you learn from the wilderness—about its value and about yourself—can guide you throughout your life. In *Mount Analog* (Penguin Books, 1974), mountaineer and author René Daumal wrote:

> You cannot stay on the summit forever; you have to come down again. . . . So why bother in the first place? Just this: What is above knows what is below, but what is below does not know what is above. . . . There is an art of finding one's direction in the lower regions by the memory of what one saw higher up. When one can no longer see, one can at least still know.

Above all, put your own ethics and opinions into action. You cannot effect change, preserve the wilderness, or expect others to adopt "leave no trace" principles unless you take action yourself. Begin by developing impeccable minimum-impact camping, traveling, and climbing practices, and be vigilant about them. Demonstrate your ethic every day. Teach it to your climbing partners and friends. Wilderness preservation can be a very simple thing that begins with you.

Bibliography

Accidents in North American Mountaineering, Jed Williamson, ed. Published annually by the American Alpine Club, New York.

American Alpine Journal, Christian Beckwith, ed. Published annually by the American Alpine Club, New York.

Bard, Dale. "Pumping Cracks." *Great Pacific Iron Works Catalog, 1978.*

Chouinard, Yvon. *Climbing Ice.* San Francisco: Sierra Club Books, 1978.

Climbing, Michael Kennedy, ed. Published bimonthly, Carbondale, CO.

Daffern, Tony. *Avalanche Safety for Skiers and Climbers.* Seattle: Cloudcap,1983.

Daumal, René. *Mount Analog.* Baltimore: Penguin Books. Inc., 1974.

Hampton, Bruce, and David Cole. *Soft Paths.* Harrisburg, PA: Stackpole Books, 1995.

Houston, Charles. *Going Higher.* Boston: Little, Brown, and Company, 1987.

Loughman, Michael. *Learning to Rock Climb.* San Francisco: Sierra Club Books, 1981.

March, Bill. *Modern Rope Techniques in Mountaineering.* Milnthorpe, England: Cicerone Press, 1990.

Mcphee, John. *Rising from the Plains.* New York: Farrar, Straus and Giroux, 1987.

Messner, Reinhold. "The Will to Survive." In *The Armchair Mountaineer,* edited by David Reuther and John Thorn. New York: Charles Scribner's Sons, 1984.

Murray, William Hutchinson. *The Scottish Himalayan Expedition.* London: J. M. Dent and Sons Ltd., 1951.

Patey, Tom. "The Art of Climbing Down Gracefully." *Mountain Magazine* 16.

Perrin, Jim, ed. *Mirrors in the Cliffs.* London: Diadem Books, Ltd., 1983.

Rebuffat, Gaston. *On Ice and Snow and Rock.* New York: Oxford University Press, 1971.

———. *The Mont Blanc Massif.* Translated by Jane and Colin Taylor. London: Oxford University Press, 1974.

Schimelpfenig, Tod, and Linda Lindsey. *NOLS Wilderness First Aid, 3rd ed.* Harrisburg, PA: Stackpole Books, 2000.

Selters, Andy. *Glacier Travel and Crevasse Rescue.* Seattle: The Mountaineers, 1990.

Setnika, Tim. *Wilderness Search and Rescue.* Boston: Appalachian Mountain Club, 1980.

Shipton, Eric. *The Six Mountain Travel Books.* London: Diadem Books, Ltd., 1985.

Tilman, H. W. *The Seven Mountain Travel Books.* London: Diadem Books, Ltd., 1983.

Walter, Tom. "A View of NOLS." *NOLS Newsletter,* April 1986.

Wilson, Ken, ed. *The Games Climbers Play.* London: Diadem Books, Ltd., 1978.

Zwinger, Ann H., and Beatrice E. Willard. *Land above the Trees.* Tucson: University of Arizona Press, 1972.

Glossary

Accessory cord Static cord made of nylon or Spectra™, used to sling protection or as cordelettes.

Acclimatizing Adapting to a new elevation or climate.

Active camming devices Camming devices that are loaded with a spring to keep them secure until loaded.

Acute Mountain Sickness (AMS) Altitude sickness with a quick onset but generally mild. Symptoms include headache, nausea, anorexia, ataxia. Commonly known as "feeling the altitude."

Aid climbing Climbing in which one makes progress or rests with the aid of artificially placed protection.

Alpine style Climbing a peak in one push, carrying all the necessary gear and food, as opposed to expedition style, which might involve ferrying loads, multiple camps, and fixed lines. Differentiated from the term alpine climb in that alpine climbs are often day climbs, while alpine style might be used on an ascent taking many days.

Anchor Protection that secures a team to the mountain.

Anchor point A point of protection.

Arete A sharp outside corner. The term originally referred to a sharp ridge formed by glacial action but now refers to any steep outside corner.

Ascender A mechanical camming device that grips the rope. It slides in one direction and grabs in the other.

Aspect The way a slope lies with respect to sun and wind.

Avalanche transceiver A device that transmits and receives a radio signal. When a buried avalanche victim's transceiver is transmitting, rescuers on the surface can receive the signal and locate the victim.

Back-clean To clean pieces of protection no longer essential to the rope system from lower on a pitch for use higher on the pitch.

Back-rope To belay a climber from below even though the climber is belayed by a top rope. This technique is most often used to help prevent swinging falls when climbers follow traversing pitches.

Belay plate (Sticht plate, Betterbrake) A piece of metal with an oval hole in it that will accept a bight of rope. When the bight is clipped to a carabiner, the tight bends in the rope supply enough friction for the human hand to hold a great deal of weight.

Belay To secure the climber with the rope.

Bend A knot that attaches two ends of rope together.

Bergschrund The highest crevasse on a glacier where the flowing ice pulls away from the stationary ice and snow above.

Bight A bend in a piece of rope.

Brakebar A friction system created with oval carabiners. Generally used for rappelling and lowering.

Brake hand The hand that actually holds rope and secures the climber. It should never leave the rope without being replaced by another hand or a tie-off.

Butterfly coil A coil made using bights in a doubled rope.

Camming device A piece of protection that rotates and multiplies force against the rock when loaded, making it very secure.

Carabiner A metal link with gates that snap closed.

Chalk Magnesium carbonate powder used by rock climbers to keep fingertips dry. Also known as "white courage."

Chock Any protection that has no moving parts and can be placed without a hammer, such as hexes, stoppers, and rp's.

Classification The difficulty rating of the hardest move of a climb. Also used to define some belay techniques, e.g., 5th Class belay.

Climate The average condition of a region's weather over a period of years determined by temperatures, winds, and precipitation.

Climb together To move over terrain roped to one's partner(s). All members of the rope team move simultaneously.

Coil A method of packaging a rope to carry.

Cordelette A piece of small-diameter accessory cord (5.5 to 7 millimeters) kept on the harness for use in improvised rescues and friction hitches.

Cornice A snow deposit on a ridge top that overhangs to the leeward.

Couloir A snow-filled gully.

Counterbalance Countering the weight of one body part with that of another, usually used to extend one's lateral reach.

Counterpressure Any combination of pushing and pulling that increases a climber's purchase by opposing forces; includes stemming and laybacking.

Cow's tail A length of webbing used to clip someone or something directly into an anchor. Often used to anchor people on multipitch rappels.

Crevasse A crack in the brittle ice of a glacier.

Crust The brittle skin of the earth, which "floats" on the molten mantle below.

Crux The most difficult move or section of a pitch or climb.

Cumulus Fluffy clouds formed by generally upward air movement.

Daisy chain A section of sling that is tied or sewn so that it offers several places to clip into. A daisy chain can be made from a chain of carabiners.

Depth hoar Snow that has metamorphosed into a weakly bonded layer buried in the snowpack. Also known as "sugar snow."

Direct transmission Electric current from lightning that is transmitted directly from an object into a person.

Directionality The direction or directions in which a piece of protection or an anchor will hold.

Double rope technique Leading on two ropes of equal length at the same time.

Dulfersitz A rappel technique that uses the body as the friction device.

Eddies Portions of slow water blocked from the main current by obstacles or by the shape of the river.

Edema Accumulation of fluid in the interstitial tissues between cells.

Edging A technique in which one places the edge of a boot on an edge of rock and stands on it.

Equalized or Equi-tension Pieces tied together in such a way that allows them to share a load.

Erosion The transport of weathered material.

Face climbing Climbing on face holds.

Fall factor A rating of the seriousness of a fall that is used to approximate the damage that may be done to the climbing rope. Fall factors range from zero to two and are calculated by dividing the total length of the fall by the amount of rope in the system at the time.

Fall line The route a falling object would take down a slope.

5th Class belay A belay in which the belayer is stationary and tied into an anchor.

Fireman's belay A back-up belay in which another person places hands on the brake rope and is ready to hold the rope if the belayer (or rappeller) lets go of it.

Firn line or firn zone A transition zone of melting snow below the snow-covered glacier and above the bare ice.

Fixed line A rope that is anchored in place along which a climber can self-belay with a friction hitch or ascender.

Flagging An extreme form of counterbalance in which one leg points off to one side to offset a long reach by the opposite hand.

Follower Any member of a rope team that does not lead the pitch.

Free-climb To make progress without placing any weight on rope systems or artificial protection.

Free-solo To free-climb alone without a belay.

Friction Resistance to motion of two moving objects or surfaces that touch. One of the four elements of a belay. Friction dissipates force, allowing the belayer's hand to hold the climber.

Friction hitch A hitch that allows one piece of rope or webbing to grab a hold on another.

Glacier travel technique Traveling roped to others but without protection in place. Stopping a fall depends completely on the position of team members, as there is no anchor.

Glacier A slow-moving river of ice.

Grade A rating of the overall commitment of a climb.

Ground current Electric current from lightning carried through the ground.

Guide biner A carabiner used to hold the climber's rope in the correct place on the belayer.

Hanging belay A stance at which the belayer's weight is fully hanging on the anchor.

High-altitude cerebral edema (HACE) Serious, acute altitude sickness that manifests itself in the skull.

High-altitude pulmonary edema (HAPE) Altitude sickness that manifests itself in the lungs, with symptoms very similar to pneumonia.

Hitch A knot that is tied around or on something else.

Hypoxia A deficiency of oxygen reaching the tissues of the body.

Icefall A heavily crevassed and steep section of glacier.

Igneous rock Rock that was crystallized from molten magma. Extrusive igneous rocks solidify near the suface of the earth and are generally related to volcanism. Intrusive igneous rocks solidify more slowly deep below the surface, and the resulting rock is very strong.

Impact force The force "felt" by a moving body as it decelerates to a stop.

Intermediate anchor Protection placed during a pitch or running belay and clipped to the rope.

Jam A camming action performed by climbers, using body parts to gain purchase in cracks.

Jug A huge face hold.

Kern The core of a kern-mantle rope. About 80 percent of a rope's strength is in the kern.

Kevlar™ A rope fiber that is strong, not elastic, and more brittle than nylon.

Kinetic energy The energy of a moving body.

Knot Any complication in a rope.

Lanyard A length of webbing from an ice ax to a climber's wrist or harness.

Lateral moraines Debris deposits that form or formed along the margin of a glacier.

Lead climber The person leading the pitch. Lead climbers climb above the belay.

Lee The side of a slope away from the direction of the wind.

Lenticular cloud A standing cloud formed when air is pushed up, quickly cools and condenses into a cloud, and then vaporizes as it warms.

Liebacking Climbing technique using counterpressure in which the climber pulls with a hand or hands and pushes with feet.

Longitudinal crevasses Crevasses that form parallel to the flow of a glacier.

Loop A closed bight.

Magic X A method for preventing an equi-tension anchor from failing if one of the protection placements fails.

Mantle The molten portion of the earth underneath the crust.

Marginal crevasses Crevasses that form along the edges of a glacier.

Mass-wasting Large-scale downslope movement of weathered material soil creep, landslide.

Medial moraines Debris dragged along the middles of glaciers.

Metamorphic rock Rock that has been chemically transformed from sedimentary or igneous by the application of heat or pressure.

Moraine Debris carried or deposited by a glacier.

Münter hitch A friction hitch that can be used as a source of friction for a belay or rappel. Also known as an Italian hitch.

Objective hazards Hazardous events caused by outside forces that happen to the climber.

Orographic weather Local mountain weather.

Palming Placing the palm of the hand on the rock and pushing.

Passive camming devices Chocks that rotate and cam when loaded but do not have springs to hold them in place.

Pendulum A swinging fall.

Perimeter The border of an area on a glacier that has been probed and determined safe for removing a belay.

Pitch The distance between two belay anchors on a 5th Class climb.

Pluck To pull debris into a glacier by freezing to it.

Point-release avalanche An avalanche begun by a small amount of snow.

Position Placement of one's body in order to increase the effectiveness of a belay.

Potential energy The energy one accumulates as one leaves the ground.

Pressure fronts The interfaces between large air masses of different air pressures.

Primary safety system The first line of defense against a fall. Movement skills are a climber's primary safety system.

Probe A long pole (15 to 20 feet long) used to probe into the snow on a glacier and determine what lies below—dense snow, a crevasse, or ice.

Protection placement Any piece of artificially placed climbing equipment that serves to secure a team to the mountain. One or more protection placements make up an anchor.

Prusik 1. A friction hitch. 2. To ascend a rope on friction hitches.

Quick draw A short (3- to 6-inch) sling or runner rigged with two carabiners.

Rack A complement of climbing protection carried by a climber.

Radial crevasses Crevasses that form like spokes on a wheel as a glacier rounds a bend.

Rappel To slide down a rope, controlling speed with friction.

Redundancy The level to which a system is backed up.

Restacking Moving a stack of rope by running the rope through one's hands.

Rime Nonprecipitated snow that accumulates on the windward sides of objects.

Roped-solo To climb alone with a rope system.

Runner 1. A shoulder sling. 2. Intermediate protection, including sling and carabiner, used to stop a fall (British).

Running belay A belay in which the entire team moves together and is held to the mountain by intermediate protection placements.

Rutchblock Test A test for snow stability in which a skier tries to create a crown fracture above a snow pit.

Sedimentary rock Rock formed from depositions of eroded material that have been buried.

Self-equalizing system A system that connects pieces of protection so that they self-adjust to changes in the direction of force and can share a load in more than one direction.

Shock load A load with velocity.

Single rope technique Climbing on a single lead rope.

Slab avalanche An avalanche that begins to slide as one cohesive layer of snow.

Sling A lenth of webbing tied or sewn into a loop.

Smear A foot technique in which as much rubber as possible is smeared onto a face hold.

Snow bridges Snow covers that span crevasses.

Solo To climb alone. The term is often used synonymously with free solo.

Spectra™ A rope fiber that is strong, not elastic, and slippery.

Spotters People meant to help a person through a section of difficulty or out of a difficult position.

Stack 1. The pile of rope not in use. 2. To put rope into a neat, manageable pile.

Stemming A counterpressure technique in which one's feet, hands, or both push in opposition.

Style The way a person climbs.

Subjective hazards Hazardous events or situations that are created or partially created by a climber or climbers.

Surface hoar Feathery crystals that form on the snow surface during cold nights. Once buried, they become dangerous potential sliding layers.

Swinging leads Trading the roles of leader and second during a climb.

Tensionless anchor An anchor whose load is dissipated in friction around a tree or similar object and does not tighten the knots involved.

Terminal moraine Debris left at the toe of a glacier.

Toe (of a glacier) The end or terminus of a glacier.

Top roping A belay that is above the climber.

Transceiver A radio that transmits and receives distress signals. Transceivers are carried by travelers in avalanche terrain and allow rescuers to locate buried victims (less than 5 or 6 feet deep) in a matter of minutes.

Transverse crevasse A crevasse that forms perpendicular to the flow of a glacier.

Weathering The breakdown of rock by the forces of nature.

Webbing Flat profile nylon.

Wedge A piece of protection that is slotted into cracks. Wedges are effective, but placements are generally good in only one direction.

Windward The side of a slope that faces the direction of the wind.

Zone of ablation The area on a glacier in which there is an annual net loss of snow cover and ice to melting.

Zone of accumulation The area on a glacier in which there is an annual net gain in snow cover and ice.

Index